For Jane

With Love

Wilhelmina Harris

Brave Little
DUTCH GIRL

Memories of a small child in Holland
during the German occupation 1940-45

Wilhelmina Harris

UNITED WRITERS
Cornwall

UNITED WRITERS PUBLICATIONS LTD
Ailsa, Castle Gate, Penzance, Cornwall.

British Library Cataloguing in Publication Data:
A catalogue record for this book is
available from the British Library.

ISBN 1 85200 106 2

Printed in Great Britain by
United Writers Publications Ltd
Cornwall.

For my sister, the brave little Dutch girl;
and for my children and grandchildren.

Acknowledgements

I would like to express my thanks to my sister, uncles and aunts and all other members of my family for their help in telling me their stories and helping me to refresh my memory.

My grateful thanks also to the Historische Vereniging Maassluis for letting me use the book *Historische Schetsen No 26*.

My gratitude to my husband for his patience and encouragement.

Contents

Contents

Prologue:

Hunger

"Be very, very careful, darling," her distressed mother said with tears of anxiety in her eyes.

"I will Mum, don't worry, lots of people go to the islands to get food, I'll be fine."

"You know what to do when they start bombing, don't you?"

"Yes Mum, I've had to lie flat on my stomach in fields before."

"Bye then sweetheart, see you tomorrow. Make sure you don't leave her until she's on that boat," she told the girl's father.

"Bye Dicky," her little five-year-old sister said as they waved her off.

It was the winter of 1944-45 in Holland. The Germans were deliberately starving the west of the country. It was bitterly cold with temperatures well below freezing point. Canals and ponds had frozen over and an icy wind made matters worse.

There was no coal or wood to keep the fires in the houses going but worst of all there was no food. The soup, which was dished out by the communal soup kitchens, was nothing but water with pieces of potato and some cabbage leaves floating unappetisingly in the large cauldrons. Black bread, which was hardly edible and not fit for human consumption, finished the meagre rations. In January 1945 the portions had gone down to half a litre of soup per person per day and the bread rations had dropped to 500 grams a week. People were dying in the streets and buried in cardboard boxes.

Dicky was twelve years old. She was quite a sturdy girl and tall for her age but underfed as everybody was at this dreadful time. She lived in the small town of Maassluis, the first town up from Hook of Holland along the river Maas, now called the New Waterway. On the other side of the river is Rozenburg, the first of the islands which form the extreme southwest of the country.

Her paternal grandparents hailed from the island of Voorne and Putten, the next island up from Rozenburg. Some of the relations, including her grandfather's sister, still lived there. There was little communication between them because of an inheritance which had been promised to her grandfather but had never materialised and had gone to other relatives. It had left a rift in the family.

Desperate for food, Dicky's father Kardien had suggested that she should go to these relations, they were farmers and were bound to have enough, even though most of it went to the Germans.

"Look, just go there, tell them who you are and explain we have nothing left to eat."

"You must be out of your mind," her mother had reacted angrily. "How will she be able to find Zwartewaal. Do you really think they will help; they haven't spoken to your parents for years. Anyway it's far too dangerous to send a little girl all the way over there on her own. What if they start bombing again, have you thought of that?"

"For God's sake Mien it's our only chance, the Germans won't harm a little girl. They're bad but not that bad. Think of our other little girl, she's skin over bone, be reasonable for once in your life."

"How is she going to get to Rozenburg? Half of Rotterdam is waiting to get to the other side in that stupid rowing boat, she might have to wait for days," her mother Mien retorted.

"I'll find a way," he said and left to go to the harbour.

*　　*　　*　　*

12

The ferry which sailed between Maassluis and Rozenburg had long since been taken over by the Germans and a large rowing boat, operated by six men on the oars, was now the only means of transport. When Dicky's father arrived at the place where the rowing boat departed from he found scores of people waiting to cross. Some had been waiting for more than twenty-four hours. He knew it was hopeless and instead went in search of the small boats that sometimes took goods over to the islands. As he knew a lot of people in the town he managed to find somebody who was willing to take her across the following morning and drop her on the island of Voorne and Putten.

"For goodness sake don't tell anybody else, otherwise other people will want to come and I'm not allowed to take passengers," the boatman had warned.

"OK and thanks, see you tomorrow morning around nine."

The next morning Dicky and her bicycle and some other people were smuggled on board and they set off across the river. Her dad had given her precise instructions on how to get to his aunt. It was going to be a long way. She had often been in search of food, but always together with a friend. Now, all on her own, she was frightened. She'd never been to Voorne and Putten before and was worried she might get lost.

Riding her bicycle, which had no proper tyres, just hard rubber strips round the wheels leaving the steel edges exposed, was hard work and very uncomfortable. People sometimes put wooden strips or hosepipe round the wheels. Only the Germans had proper tyres on their bikes.

Only a small part of the river could be used because right from the start of the war mines had been dropped, leaving only the crossing between Maassluis and Rozenburg free, so that the Germans could move freely from the mainland to the islands.

When they reached the other side they had to stay very close to the shore to avoid the mines. They went round the island of Rozenburg, but when they eventually reached the landing stage in Voorne the Germans told the captain to clear off. He didn't dare make a fuss for the sake of the illegal passengers who were hidden below deck.

"We'll have to try a bit further on, they won't let us come in," the boatman told them.

Dicky was now more frightened then ever.

"If we are going to be dropped somewhere else I won't know the way, my dad told me how to get to my aunt but now I will get lost," she sobbed.

"Where do you have to go to lass?" a woman asked her.

"To Zwartewaal."

"Best to ask when we get there, let's see first if we can make it at all."

After what seemed like hours, they finally got off in the middle of nowhere. On her ramshackle bicycle she set off. It was freezing hard and her so-called winter coat and hand-knitted mittens were totally inadequate for this weather. A large woollen scarf covered her dark shoulder-length hair.

Darkness was already falling and she had no idea where she was. She struggled with her bike through an endless frozen field until she eventually reached a farmhouse. She knocked on the door and a friendly woman put her on the right road. She cycled past frozen, barren fields, past farmhouses which looked all but deserted. She asked passers-by for directions several times, eventually reaching the tiny village of Zwartewaal. By then she was frozen, desperately hungry, close to tears and she had no idea where to find the aunt. Luckily she saw a man approaching and asked him.

"Sir, do you know where the farm of the family Hoftijzer is?"

"Good Lord girl, where have you come from? You look half frozen to death."

"I've come from Maassluis. You see we have nothing left to eat and I've come to ask if my aunt can spare us some. I left home at nine this morning and I've had nothing to eat."

"You poor little mite. Yes I know where your aunt lives, I'll show you."

"Thank you sir, is it far?"

"No, only about five minutes."

When she reached the house it was so dark that she could not make out if it was big or small, but the front door was brightly painted and looked quite inviting. Still frightened that they might send her away, she rang the doorbell. A middle-aged, quite stern looking lady opened the door.

"Yes?" she said in a rather unfriendly way.

"Um, I am Dicky van der Hoek, Kardien's daughter, I've come all the way from Maassluis. We have no food left and my dad wondered if you could help us. He thought maybe you have a little something to spare. We are all starving, including my five-year-old sister," she blurted out fighting back the tears.

"Oh, I see, well I don't know, just wait here a minute." She went back to the living-room and left Dicky shivering on the doorstep. She didn't know what she was going to do if they sent her away. Tears started to run down her cheeks. She was terrified and had never felt so alone.

"You'd better come in and see my mother, she is your grandfather's sister," the woman said when she returned to the door.

When Dicky walked into the room old aunt Anna folded her in her arms as if she was the prodigal daughter.

"Oh, darling girl, look at you, cycled all the way from Maassluis in this weather, you poor lamb. You look half dead. We'll get some food into you and then you must tell me all about the family. How is your grandmother and all the children? It's so wonderful to see you. Take your coat off and sit by the fire."

Dicky was quite overwhelmed by it all and very relieved that she had not been sent packing.

It was nice and warm in the room, which was stuffed with furniture. The thick curtains were tightly closed and a few small paraffin lamps burned brightly, making it look safe and comforting. Aunt Anna looked like somebody out of a fairy tale in her long black clothes and her white cotton cap, which was fastened with a bow under her chin, perched on her grey hair.

The daughter, who had opened the door to her, was sent to the kitchen to fetch hot milk and bread.

A little while later aunt Anna's son arrived and of course he was told the whole story.

"You'd better come home with me for the night. We've got a spare bed and I can then help you on your way tomorrow.

Dicky, not forgetting what the aim of her journey was, asked, "Aunt Anna, do you think you could spare us maybe some potatoes and flour? My little sister is so thin and my mum is really worried and we have nothing to eat but the soup from the kitchens and the foul bread. Sometimes, if we're lucky, we have some sugarbeets."

"Oh God, you poor devils, we knew it was bad in that part of the country, but we didn't know it was that bad. We don't have that much here now, most of the crop and milk is taken by the Germans, but at least we're not starving yet and of course we'll give you some food, and you can come to us again if necessary. Now I think you should go home with my son and have a good night's sleep. Give everybody my love but your grandma in particular." They kissed goodbye and Dicky thanked them for their kindness.

The following morning her bike was loaded up with so much food that she could hardly ride it. They gave her 10 kilos of brown beans, 10 kilos of dried peas, flour, at least 10 kilos of potatoes, eggs and a small piece of bacon. The son took her to a small rowing boat that acted as a ferry between Voorne and Rozenburg and going this way would make her journey considerably shorter. She had to unload the bicycle before going on the boat and re-load it again on the other side. She tried very hard to put it all back on, but it was just too difficult and heavy for her. She was desperate, she had to take it all with her. The boatman who saw her struggle came to help her and suggested she leave the potatoes behind.

"But I can't, we've got nothing to eat, I must take it all with me," she cried.

"Look darling, you'll never manage with that load, don't forget you have to unload it all again when you get to the boat in Rozenburg. I'll look after your spuds and you can come and collect them another time."

"You won't eat them will you?" she asked him anxiously.

16

"No lass, they will be here waiting for you, I promise."

He was true to his word because her father retrieved them a few days later. Food in the rural communities was also scarce but they were not starving like the people in the towns across the river.

Full of a good breakfast, she happily cycled across the island of Rozenburg to the place where the rowing boat was to take her back to Maassluis. She arrived there at about 10.30 in the morning and found the most enormous queue waiting to cross. Her heart sank. The rowing boat only took a few people across at a time and it would be hours before it would be her turn.

She sat down beside her overloaded bicycle and waited. It was a freezing cold day but she had to stay close to her bike otherwise her food would have been stolen.

She ate the bread which she had been given for the journey. Some people looked enviously at her bundles and she became more and more worried that they would take it from her.

The whole ferry operation was overseen by a very grumpy, very fat German, who would rant and rave every time the passengers were scrambling to get on board. He treated the people as if they were animals. Nobody dared say a word against him though, for fear of not being let onto the boat at all. A shiver went through all the people every time he opened his mouth.

When six o'clock came and the last boat was loading Dicky knew she would not get on and now faced the prospect of having to stay either outside the whole night or in the dreadful shed, which stood near the landing place and where people who could not get across were allowed to stay. She was petrified and knew she had to do something. Luckily she was endowed with considerable acting talents. She opened her mouth and began to sob very loudly. A kind woman, who had a place on the last boat heard her.

"Oh, you poor little girl, you can't stay here all night, I'll tell you what, you take my place. I have relations here and can go back to them, I'll try again tomorrow."

"Thank you ever so much, you see my dad will be waiting for me and if I don't get home my mum will be frightened to death."

"OK, lovey, now let's unload the bike."

All the stuff had to come off once more. The bikes were put in a heap, one on top of the other to save space, at one end of the boat and the ten or so passengers huddled together at the other end, staying close to the treasures they had managed to get.

Finally she reached Maassluis again where her father was waiting for her. When her dad loaded everything back on the bike, the eggs were missing, stolen by one of the other passengers. That's how desperate the people were.

This brave little Dutch girl, who made the trip twice more, was my sister.

The Dutch population suffered terrible hardships through the five years of being occupied by the Germans. To me it was all quite normal because from the day I was conceived war was inevitable.

1

The Start

At the time of my appearance the world was a turbulent place. I was born on the day that Franco's Nationalist Troops walked into Barcelona. He had the full support of Nazi Germany and when his forces entered Madrid at the end of March congratulations were sent to him by Hitler and Italy's Mussolini. Germany was once more a threat to the stability of Europe. Hitler had become a byword for terror and war was thought to be imminent.

My father, mother and six-year-old sister lived in a small, rented house in Maassluis. The river, which forms part of the port of Rotterdam and is now the busiest port in the world, has always been the most important feature of the town. Maassluis used to be a thriving fishing town, but as with everywhere else, times changed and in the late 1930s fishing vessels in the harbour had made way for the large tugs of Smit and Co. It had also become the home of the pilot boats. However, some fishing activities still remained in those days.

Our house, which was always spotlessly clean, was a typical labourer's house. It had two small rooms, one for living in and the posh front room which was only used for special occasions.

The living-room had lino on the floor with a carpet on top that was just big enough for the table, the four chairs and two carvers to stand on. The seats of these wooden chairs were covered in some kind of brown artificial leather. There was always a nice woollen tablecloth on the table with a bunch of flowers or a pot plant in the middle. Our sideboard had two cupboards and two drawers and on top of that was another smaller part with glass doors, which housed the glasses, all nicely arranged by size. On the mantelpiece were some cheap ornaments, and plants, mostly geraniums, decorated the windowsill.

My mother had this knack for making things look pretty and our little house always looked very cheerful. A few pictures had been arranged around the walls and some valueless, but nice, little ornaments stood on the sideboard.

There was a small kitchen which incorporated the toilet in the corner. My mother cooked on a two-burner gas hob and paraffin burners were used for simmering.

Upstairs was one bedroom in which my sister slept and later also housed my cot, and the large space directly on top of the narrow stairs where my parent's bed and the large wardrobe stood. The beds were always made up with crisp white sheets and not a speck of dust was ever to be found on the linoleum that covered the floors.

High up around this space was the loft, where the Christmas decorations were kept and all other stuff we didn't use at the time. We had no bathroom. Bathing was done, once a week, in a sink tub in the kitchen, and when it was too cold in winter, in front of the fire in the living-room.

The window in the living-room looked out on the small yard at the back. There was a shed where the bicycles and the sink tubs were kept. On Mondays, when the weather was fine, my mother would do the washing outside, otherwise she did it in the shed.

The whites had to be soaked overnight in washing soda then rinsed the next day and then pounded in hot soapy water, then rinsed again and put through blue water and then some of them had to be starched. The dark clothes were just pounded and scrubbed on the washing board. After being put through the wringer the washing was hung to dry on the lines that were suspended between the two walls. When everything was dry all was carefully ironed, including all the underwear.

There were two rabbit hutches, one on top of the other, which contained a rabbit each. They used to mysteriously disappear around Christmas-time. I was always told that they had escaped and that we would get some new ones. I was never told where the delicious Christmas dinner rabbit on my plate came from. Maybe I had my suspicions but I never asked. I was probably afraid to hear the truth. In due course two little ones duly appeared to replace the 'escaped' ones.

The window in the front room looked out onto the road and towards the dyke.

The estate on which we lived, consisted of three small streets situated at right angles from our street with a square at the other end followed by another large estate. To the right of the square the farmland started. On the corner of our street and the street where my paternal grandparents lived, was a corner shop, which became an important part in my young life. On the corner of the next street was the greengrocer and on the next the butcher. This shop became a soup kitchen in the hunger winter of 1944-45.

Maassluis had, and still has, two canals. Each with a sluice that is opened when the water in the canals becomes too high. On the other side of the sluices is the inner harbour. The canals are fed by the water which is constantly pumped by means of small windmills from the farmland to keep it dry.

The inner harbour flows into the outer harbour and then into the New Waterway, which empties its waters into the North Sea in Hook of Holland.

The market square sits right in the middle of the town in between the two canals below the dyke. The canal on the north side of the market is called North Canal and the other one the South Canal. The market place has always been a really cosy place with nice, friendly shops and in my young days there was a café where cups of coffee and tea and ice creams were sold. There was also a large bookshop, the apothecary and various other shops all built around the square. Later, many years after the war, the very popular weekly market was held right in the middle.

Along the canals were also lots of shops; there were then shoe

21

shops, clothes shops, the photographer, cake shops, butchers and a large furniture store. The greengrocer shop of my Uncle Harry and Aunt Nel, my father's sister, was, in those days, along the South Canal. A bridge over this canal leads you from the market into a very narrow street, called New Street, that is crammed full with mainly small shops.

In my young days there was the Co-op, which was quite a large grocery store. There was a bakery, a florist, a haberdashery, a men's clothing shop, a newsagent, a chemist, a greengrocer and a very posh jeweller. This shop was so posh that you felt you had to take your shoes off before you entered. I remember going in there with my mother once and I hardly dared to speak. It was still the same many years later when, for my sixteenth birthday, I went there, again with my mum, to buy my first gold ring. At that time the eldest daughter of my Aunt Nel worked there. However, she was very kind, she was also incredibly posh. She managed to talk while hardly opening her mouth. It made her look as if she was pouting all the time. I thought it was rather silly but maybe that was the posh fashion in those days.

On entering the shop you had the feeling that you had stepped into some sort of temple where one was allowed in only by the grace of God. The lighting was quite dim apart from above the counter where there was a special bright light so you could actually see what you were buying. The carpet was so thick that no sound was made when you walked on it. It was really all a bit unnerving. You had the feeling that if you didn't buy anything, unseen hands would silently grab you until you had made a purchase. It was pretty creepy actually. Even at the age of sixteen I was pleased when I had chosen a ring and could escape outside to take a good deep breath again.

The bridge at the beginning of New Street has always played a big part in the gossip of the town and up to this day you can find people congregating there for a daily natter as they have done for centuries.

Walking through this street, away from the canal, brings you to the part where we lived.

In Maassluis you live either 'under' or 'on top' of the dyke.

The town is completely split in half by the one dyke that runs from Hook of Holland to Rotterdam and beyond. Our little house sat right under this dyke in the large housing estate which is built in a polder and which is neatly surrounded by more dykes.

At the very end of our road was the cinema-cum-theatre, where my mother performed with her amateur dramatics society.

On the other side of the river is Rozenburg, then still an island where farmers thrived. The outskirts now house large oil refineries and all sorts of industries. This part has been re-named Pernis and belongs to Rotterdam.

A ferry was the only means of transport to and from the island. The area of the town, from where the ferry sails and also the enormous housing estate, is called 'The Head' and people from all over town used to take a stroll there on a Sunday afternoon to see all the activities on the river.

The large dyke rose right in front of us, separated only by a pavement and a small road. It was also this dyke which prevented thousands and thousands of people from drowning when, in the massive floods of February 1st 1953, the water came to less than half a metre from the edge. If it had gone over, half of the country would have perished. Every single house, from the river's edge right to the top of the dyke, was flooded in this dreadful disaster. The province of Zeeland was hardest hit. A total of 400,000 acres was flooded and 1,800 people lost their lives. The loss of livestock was catastrophic. Now with the Delta Project finished, floods like these can never happen again. Massive dams and sluices, built in between the islands of Zeeland, now regulate the flow of the waters.

To get to the top of the dyke from where we lived you either have to use the concrete steps, which you find all over the town or, if travelling on wheels, go up the gentle slopes.

As Holland is as flat as a pancake and no hills are to be found, in winter, when snow had fallen, the slopes formed excellent places to slide down aided by a cardboard box, a piece of carpet or, if you were lucky, a sledge.

*   *   *   *

My father, Kardien, worked on the spinning machines in a local factory, where they made rope and carpets. We were not really poor, but money was tight. Both my parents were avid socialists and both worked very hard to improve the welfare of the working class. My mother used to go to conferences for women's rights, which was still quite unusual in those days and many people saw them as a very modern and progressive couple. My father was a staunch unionist and would risk his own job for the sake of others. Heated conversations were often heard in our house and many a threat uttered towards their bosses. It shaped my life and I will still mostly take the side of the underdog.

Sport was very important in those days and the carpet factory had their own football and gymnastic club where my mother won many a prize for various facets of the sport. She also trained the little children.

The football club, in which my father and two of his brothers played, still exists today.

My mother didn't work, that was not done in those days, but she was always busy knitting or sewing or cleaning. She had been in service from the age of fourteen. My parents married when she was twenty-three and my father twenty-five. It hadn't been an easy courtship.

My mother's father, Eerde van Teylingen, was killed when she was 11. At the time he was the captain of the *Cornelia Clasina*, a ship filled with 130,000kg of carbide. They had moored in one of the harbours in Rotterdam the night before the fatal accident.

The next morning, according to the newspaper of November 19th 1917, most of the crew had left the vessel to go home to their families but because of the intake of some water the pumps were still running. Captain van Teylingen had been called to the telephone on the shore and had left the ship. One of the remaining crew members went down below deck with an oil lamp to check on the pumping progress. When my grandfather returned to the vessel it exploded, throwing him up into the air. He was later found in the hold of the lighter which was moored next to his ship. He died on the way to hospital. He was thirty-six years old.

The explosion was so enormous that it could be heard in the

24

centre of Rotterdam. The upper part of the vessel had been completely blown apart and debris was later found all around the harbour. Windows in warehouses and other buildings in the area had been blown out. Even when the vessel had already sunk the carbide kept burning and it took many hours to control it. It was one of the worst accidents ever to happen in any of the Rotterdam harbours.

My mother used to wear a wide, gold ring that had belonged to her father and was supposedly found embedded in his head.

She adored her dad and on that fatal day was, as always, waiting for him at the railway station in Maassluis. The station chef who knew her from the numerous times she'd been collecting her dad and who must have been informed of the tragedy, told her:

"You'd better go home lovey, your daddy is not coming."

"But of course he's coming, he will be on the next train, he's just a bit delayed, that's all, he will be sad when he arrives and I'm not here, I always wait for him."

"No darling, he's not coming, you'd better go to your mum."

He did eventually persuade her and when she arrived home rather bewildered she was told the dreadful news. She was devastated. She had idolised her father and she often told us stories about him. He was a bit of an adventurer and an irrepressible optimist, a trait my mother inherited from him. He could be a bit irresponsible sometimes, but he always earned good money. One of his jobs took the whole family to England and they lived in Great Yarmouth for the best part of a year, where he was the buyer of fish for a large company.

After this tragic accident her mother was left with six children and her behaviour became somewhat unconventional. A little girl was born with father unknown and later a little boy. My mother couldn't cope with that and left home. She never lost contact with her siblings, however.

My father's family was very decent and upright. My grandfather was a cooper and they were very poor, but all ten children were

b

always clean, well behaved and taught the rights and wrongs of life. It was a wonderful family, although they were sometimes a bit narrow-minded.

In this small town tales of bad behaviour spread fast and having an illegitimate child was a terrible scandal never to be forgotten or forgiven. So when they discovered that my father was courting my mother there was hell to pay and my grandmother told him in no uncertain terms that nothing could come of it.

"You will immediately stop seeing that girl, her mother is a good for nothing, I will not have her daughter in my house."

"For goodness sake mother, she hasn't lived at home for years. She is in decent service, she can't help what her mother is like. I love her and I won't give her up."

"You do as you're told my lad, otherwise you can leave this house."

"I will not give her up. Ask Jan, he knows her and he likes her."

Jan, his brother, took his side and spoke up for the girl, without success.

"I will not discuss it any further, she is not coming into this family and that's the end of it."

When he wanted to go out that night to see my mother, he could not find his shoes. His mother or one of his sisters had hidden them.

As often happens, they had to accept her in the end and she became my grandmother's favourite daughter-in-law. None of my mother's family attended the wedding. Apparently her mother made trouble on their wedding day, but this story was never revealed to us. My mother still kept in contact with her brothers and sister, but I was about eight when I saw my maternal grandmother for the first time. By then the illegitimate daughter, Tiny, had married and had her first baby. Houses were still in very short supply after the war and she lived with her mother. My mother was determined to go and see her and after a terrible row with my father we cycled to Vlaardingen where my grandmother now lived.

After that my grandmother visited us occasionally but it was never very successful because my father couldn't stand the sight of her. I really liked her because you could have such a laugh with her. Aunt Tiny's husband was a wonderful chap and when they eventually moved to The Hague I often went to stay with them and my parents used to visit them regularly. Isn't it odd how things turn out in life.

When my mother fell pregnant with me, my parents were delighted. My sister was already nearly six and they were getting worried that it would never happen again.

"I hope it will be a boy," my father said. "We'll call him Kardien, after my father and myself." He ran straight over to his parents who lived only a couple of minutes away.

"Guess what Mother, Mien is at last pregnant again, it will hopefully be a boy this time." My grandmother, who herself had given birth to ten children, was delighted, even though I was to be her twelfth grandchild.

"Let's just pray it will be healthy and be born in peace," was her typical reaction.

The name Kardien exists only in our family. When my grandfather was born he had to be named after an old cousin whose name was Katerina. As the baby happened to be a boy they changed this name to Kardinus. The eldest sons of my father's brothers are all called this and he was very keen to carry on with the tradition but he had to wait until my own son was born to see the name live on.

Times were worrying. Germany was yet again turning into a threat. Hitler was becoming more and more powerful. 'This bloody Hitler bloke' became the main subject of conversations, interspersed with arguments about football, the love of my father's life.

When Hitler moved his troops into Sudetenland, part of Czechoslovakia, on October 5th 1938, tempers ran high.

"What the hell does he think he's doing just walking into somebody else's territory, he's becoming far too big for his boots, bloody mad Austrian," my father would rant to his friends. Just over a month later, on November 9th, the horror of the Crystal Night followed.

"Oh God, did you hear what happened in Germany Mien?" asked my father when he came home from work.

"Yes, I heard it on the radio. It's frightening what they are doing to the Jews. They're just killing them indiscriminately and destroying their businesses. It just doesn't bear thinking about."

"Just being a Jew, even in other countries, must frighten the life out of you. I wonder what butcher van Gelderen must be thinking. I wonder if he has any relatives in Germany. It's unbelievable what people can do to each other. I don't know what the hell they're going to do next."

"What do you think Kardien, will there be a war? I'm really worried, even more now with this baby on the way."

"Well don't you worry about that now, if a war comes about, we will probably be neutral again, the same as in the last war. What does big mouth Hitler want with such a small country anyway? No, we'll be all right. You know what happened in the First World War, we never got involved.

Did my father himself believe what he said or did he just say it to reassure my mother? Whichever way his statement couldn't have been more wrong. My father followed every move on the radio and discussions with friends and family were centred on this subject.

I was due on February 25th 1939, on my father's birthday. On the evening of the January 25th my mother felt unwell.

"I think I'm getting the flu Kardien, I don't feel very well at all."

"Why? Do you feel cold or have you got a headache or something?"

"No, pains in my stomach, I just feel awful, I think I'll go to bed." A few hours later she discovered the cause of her 'flu'; I was born within half an hour at three o'clock in the morning of January 26th 1939.

The hoped for son was me and I was christened Wilhelmina Elisabeth Adriana van der Hoek after my mother and my father's unmarried sister.

I was welcomed into a large, loving family, which played a massive role in my life and whose stories still enthral my children and grandchildren.

2

The Family

The first people I learned to know in my young life, apart from my parents and sister, were my father's parents. I remember my grandmother vividly, a small sturdy woman, sitting in her high-backed carver chair, always dressed in long black or dark grey clothes, thick black stockings and a black and white patterned apron. It made no difference if it was winter or summer; she always wore the same things. With her feet firmly planted on a low footstool, she always had a basket on her lap. In it were either clothes to be mended or vegetables to be cleaned. Her hair was completely white and quite thin and was pulled back from her face to end in a small bun at the back of her neck. She was not a particularly sweet old lady, but was always interested in you and would make time to listen to your stories. We all adored her.

My grandfather, who I only knew for a very short time, always sat opposite her on the other side of the table, in his own carver. He was very often chewing tobacco and at regular intervals spat a dark brown liquid into a spittoon, which stood in the corner next to his chair out of everybody's sight. He was a very kind man with very pale blue eyes and he always seemed to be smiling.

He had worked hard all his life as a cooper; sometimes until eleven o'clock at night at the height of the herring season, making the barrels for the fish brought into Maassluis by the trawlers. At the end of the week there was no money left for food and

Grandma had to go shopping as soon as Grandpa would arrive home with the wages, even if it was very late at night. Some of the shops stayed open really late because they knew women were waiting for their men to bring the money home.

For a little while he went to work in Germany as a cooper where they could earn a lot more, but it was too hard for my grandmother to cope with all those children on her own, and they decided that it was better to have less money and all be together. His only hobby was fishing and many a time a catch of fresh eel would feed the ever-growing family. Retirement was unheard of in those days and he worked until he was seventy years old.

They had a hard life bringing up their offspring, which consisted of seven boys and three girls, born between 1888 and 1913. My grandmother fell pregnant with her last child when she was forty-seven. She was so ashamed of the fact that she was pregnant at her age that she hardly dared go out to do her shopping and my grandfather had to endure many a jibe from his work mates.

Life became a lot easier when all the children started earning and paid towards the household costs. To make it all even better, years later, my Uncle Adriaan with the help of his sister Nel's husband Harry, managed to buy the house they were living in and they were secretly very proud of the fact that they lived in their 'own' home.

All except uncles Adriaan and Jo and Aunt Bep were married with children by the time I was born, my eldest cousin being already twenty-three. Two weeks after me another Wilhelmina van der Hoek was born, the daughter of my father's younger brother Arie and his wife Alida. We both attended the same primary school after the war and to stop confusion we were called little and large as my cousin was much bigger than me.

Most of my father's siblings lived in Maassluis except for two who lived in Vlaardingen, the next town up along the river, and one who lived in America. He was one of the older boys and a sailor at the time World War I broke out. They were in America around that time and his captain, who knew Holland had mobilised its troops, advised him to leave the ship to avoid military service, as war seemed inevitable. He was also married with two children and lived in New York. They never saw him again. Just before his planned visit to Holland he died.

On special days such as Saint Nicholas or New Year's Eve the biggest part of the family would descend on my grandparents and the unmarried daughter Elisabeth (Bep for short) would be cooking and baking in the tiny kitchen which was mainly taken up by the kitchen range. She would also think up all sorts of games to play and one day it was proverbs.

"Let's play who knows the most proverbs. You start Kardien, and then we go round clockwise."

The first rounds were easy but every time they got stuck my aunt would say, "Must just go to the kitchen and see to the food." While there she kept shouting, "I know another one," and putting on her most dramatic voice recited the little gem.

"Gosh Bep, that was a good one, where do you get them from?" the other participants asked.

"Oh, just sudden inspiration." She had to be in the kitchen rather a lot at that stage.

When they were all leaving to go home, they found her 'inspiration'. There on the table in the little passageway lay a special little book with every proverb in existence in it. They all thought it was hilarious but they never let her forget her dishonesty.

Their house was on the far corner of the street that was at a right angle to ours. It was a little bigger than ours. They had three bedrooms, a front room and a living-room that had a large alcove which had housed the cupboard-bed where my grandparents slept when all the children were still at home. In the daytime the doors of this bed were shut. Inside on the wall was a shelf where the newborn baby would sleep in a basket.

The girls occupied one bedroom and the boys were crammed into the other two, where they slept three or four to a double bed. There was no bathroom. They all had to wash themselves in the minuscule kitchen. It was so small that it didn't even fit a sink tub; so bathing was done in the bedrooms or in the summer in the shed, which was in the small, walled garden.

31

Bathing in a bedroom could be a rather hazardous affair as my youngest uncle found out once. Having stepped out of the tub he then sat on the rim and the whole thing tipped up and soaked everything in sight.

They had two entrances, the front door and a door that led into the garden. Every day when my father walked home from the factory he would walk through the garden entrance through the kitchen, open the living-room door and shout:

"Hello Mum, Dad, everything OK?"

"Yes, fine lad. Had a good day?"

"Yes, fine thanks. Must get home, see you." And then walk straight out again through the front door.

At birthdays the whole family would be together, all the brothers huddled in the alcove. The conversation would grow louder and louder, the whole family being endowed with very loud voices. The subjects they talked about were always in the same order. First came politics and then football.

Uncle Jan, my father and Uncle Arie were footballers and they all played in the same team. Arie, a very large beefy sort of person and the biggest of the whole bunch, was an excellent player and was called 'the canon' because he could shoot with so much strength that some goalkeepers would not play if he was in the team.

"I'm not playing in goal when he's playing, he shoots straight through you," was one of the comments once uttered by a goalie. Once he was asked to play for the Dutch football team. He would have loved to do that, but it was in the thirties, in the middle of the depression. He was unemployed at the time and could not afford the train fare to Rotterdam, which he had to pay himself. In those days the players didn't get paid or even their expenses reimbursed, it was just an honour to play for your country. It's rather different in this day and age.

My father, Adriaan and Arie were always called the triplets because they were very close in age and mostly dressed in the same Sunday suits made by my eldest Aunt Truus who was a seamstress. She earned a good living making clothes for other people, but also saw to it that all the members of the family were dressed properly.

Aunt Bep was a remarkable storyteller and I would often ask, "Please aunt, tell me the stories of the three boys."

"OK, come and sit close to me then."

I would snuggle up to her, ears at the ready.

"Well, Arie, Adriaan and your dad were nearly all the same size. Aunt Truus, who could sew beautifully, would make them the most wonderful sailor suits, which they wore on a Sunday to go to church. They only had two sets of clothes you see, one for going to school, which had to be washed over the weekend, and one for Sunday. They all had to go to church but sometimes they would sneak out after breakfast and go and play in the fields near the house. What they liked best was jumping ditches. There were plenty of those of course, as they divide all the farmer's fields. After the rain they were full of water, but even in dry weather they were never really empty. They would take a run and jump, but sometimes one of them missed, mostly Adriaan, but sometimes your dad or Arie. Soaking wet and filthy they would arrive home, cowering by the garden door or sometimes crying so loudly that the whole street could hear it. Grandma would arrive with her slipper in her hand and shout: 'You stupid boys, how many times have you been told not to go to the fields before church. Get in the shed, the lot of you.' She would shove them in and each would get a hard smack on their bottoms with the slipper. The wet one was ordered to take his clothes off and the other two despatched to church.

" 'You'd better pray very hard and don't you dare muck about, I'll ask you about the sermon when you get home.'

" 'Yes Mum, sorry Mum, we won't do it again.' And they would slope off exuding guilt. But a few weeks later it would happen all over again. When it was Adriaan, who was so very different from all the other boys, she would always blame the other two.

" 'I've often told you not to let Adriaan jump, he's not as good at that sort of thing,' And she would smack Arie and Kardien just a little harder."

"What happened then Aunt, did they have to stay in the shed

33

all day?"

"Well, not all day. In the winter they were sent to bed. They could not be walking around in their underwear you see, because that was not done in our house, that was not proper and they had no other clothes to put on."

When I heard this story for the first time, I cried, just thinking of a poor little boy lying in a cold shed with nothing on. But I learned later that they were always kept warm and fed and dressed into something which didn't quite fit and was certainly not suitable to be seen in on a Sunday, or not in my grandma's house anyway.

Uncle Adriaan, who was the middle one of those three boys, was indeed, and always remained, totally different from all the others. He was the only one who wanted to study. When his mother asked him what he wanted for his twelfth birthday he said, "I don't want anything, no present, no party."

"What do you mean you don't want a present, don't be silly, of course you want a present."

"No I don't Mum, all I want is to go to secondary school. All I want is to study."

My grandparents were stunned but could not give in to his wishes. It was very difficult for them but they would not make any difference between the children. None of the others had ever been given a chance to further their education. It was not that they were stupid, far from it, but only well-off people could afford these luxuries. In their circles children were expected to start work as soon as they left school. Aunt Truus had managed to learn to sew, but in her spare time.

Poor Adriaan had to start earning money. He was lucky enough, after a short spell as a messenger boy, to be taken on as an apprentice clerk in a shipping agency in Maassluis. He worked very hard at night studying French, English, German and bookkeeping and he eventually reached the position of company secretary.

He never married but he became the pillar of the family and if there was ever a problem Uncle Adriaan was always the one to be consulted and he would try his utmost to find a solution.

He spoke very posh Dutch, had really classy, but wonderful, friends and played tennis, which in those days was very upmarket. He never had ideas above his station, though, and he was a wonderful son to his parents.

When he was already well into his eighties, he told my husband, still in beautiful English, about his first visit to London as a young man.

"It was an enormous adventure for me to go to London and when I stood in front of 10 Downing Street I said to myself, here I am, Adriaan van der Hoek from Maassluis, staying in London. I was so overcome with happiness that I wept."

He contrasted sharply with all the other members of the family but nobody ever mentioned it. To the whole family he was just Adriaan, a loved and highly respected member of the family.

My grandparents were very honest people and would never accept anything unless it was paid for. My poor Aunt Bep found that out quite early on in her life.

One day she was sent to the butcher. While waiting for her turn to be served she overheard two women talking about having babies:

"That subject was totally taboo in our household, however many there were born, you never mentioned it or asked about it as a child," she related in one of her other stories.

"I was so engrossed in trying to listen that I did not hear the butcher say, 'Yes girl can I help you?' Apparently he said it about three times. The fourth time he shouted it out so loud that I nearly jumped out of my skin. He asked me if I was deaf. Not wanting to say that I was listening to the women's conversation I said, yes.

" 'Have you been deaf long?' he asked in a very loud voice. Again I didn't know what to say so I just said yes.

" 'Well,' he said, 'I have a very good cure for that. I'll give you a nice piece of really fatty bacon and when you go to bed tonight put it on your ear, wrap a scarf round it to keep it in place and you'll see by tomorrow morning you'll be hearing much better.'

" 'Oh, thank you,' I said. When I came home and my mother found the piece of bacon she wanted to know, of course, where that had come from. I told her that I hadn't heard the butcher and that when he asked if I was deaf I'd said yes but I omitted the bit about the women and their conversation. She was furious.

" 'You ridiculous little girl, you're not deaf, you were dreaming again I suppose as usual, how dare you bring this family into disrepute by saying you're deaf. You can go and take this piece back and tell the butcher the truth, you stupid child.' I had to do it and I felt the biggest fool in the world. I suppose I could have just thrown the piece away but not obeying my mother was such a sin that I did not even contemplate this option."

Rules were strict in the house. Swearing, belching and farting were out of the question, but when the boys were older they would stand up, go to the living-room door, fart and then run off upstairs. My grandmother's slipper would always make a loud bang against the closed door. When they grew up, swearing became quite the norm. However, in their parents company they tried hard not to do it too often.

Grandma really was one for keeping up appearances. She wasn't a snob but certain things were just not done. I have always loved the tale that my father told me about his underwear.

"When I was engaged to your mother we were going to stay with her aunt in Scheveningen. I bought myself a new set of underwear for the occasion. When my mother found out she was enraged.

" 'You're not taking brand new underwear with you my lad, what must people think, that you don't have decent things to take, that your old stuff isn't fit to see the light of day. No my boy, it will have to be washed first.'

"Who was going to see my underwear I don't know, but washed it was."

We still say these things in the family now. If somebody is deaf or pretending to be deaf we'll ask, "Have you tried bacon?" When I go on holiday and pack my new bras and knickers I always think of my father's story but I'll happily pack it all unwashed. What complicated lives they lived in those days.

Grandma was a good and kind person, however. Her eighty-five-year-old widowed mother lived with Grandma's oldest sister, Neel, on one of the islands. One very cold winter's day she made the long and difficult trip to go and visit her. Neel, who only had two children, was rather posh and not a very kind woman. She told my grandma in no uncertain terms that she no longer wished to look after her mother.

"It's just too much I can't cope with her. She needs help with washing and dressing and anyway my two daughters are fed up with it too. She'll have to go somewhere else."

My grandmother took one look at her beloved, frail little mother and said, "Pack a suitcase Neel, I'll take her home with me."

Neel didn't argue, nor ask if she had a bed for her. She just packed some clothes and handed them to Grandma. With a suitcase in one hand and her old mother on her other she made the long journey back home. In the small house with all those children they gave her the front room and she lived very happily and contented for another ten years. There is no need to say that the sisters didn't speak to each other for years.

As it happened Neel herself didn't end her days as happily as her mother did. During the war the Germans evicted her from her house and occupied it themselves, which was quite commonplace. It made no difference if you were old, infirm or had anywhere else to live. If they wanted your house, that was it, they just took it, furniture and all.

She went to live in a boarding-house near her daughter, who was a teacher in Amsterdam, but during the hunger winter the landlady had no means of feeding her guests. She informed the daughter of her predicament, but the daughter did nothing to alleviate the problem. In the end the landlady transported her to an old people's home where she died from hunger, a sad and lonely old lady.

My father's family were seen as the most decent and smart people in the entire street. So much so that a little girl asked Adriaan while they were playing:

"Your parents are rich, aren't they?"

When he asked his mother about it her answer was, "Yes son, we are rich."

Even though it was not money-wise she must have felt a rich

person with ten healthy children and a hardworking husband.

On May 4th 1939 it was Grandma's birthday and the whole family had gathered together. The mood was sombre. On April 10th Holland had placed its troops along the German border.

"What do you think Jan, is there going to be a war?" my dad asked his elder brother.

"I bloody hope not, but it doesn't look good, does it? Bloody Hitler has taken over Austria, Czechoslovakia, part of Lithuania, has Italy dancing to his tune, and they're now in Albania."

"Don't forget Spain is on his side as well. I'll tell you everybody at work is worried sick and afraid that Hitler might try to get a foothold here. I mean putting troops along the border must indicate the government is worried," added Arie.

"Yes, well," said Jan. "Don't forget that I was mobilised for four years during the First World War and nothing ever happened, so putting soldiers there doesn't really mean that much."

"Come off it mate, we didn't have bloody Hitler in the First World War. This bloke is power mad, well just mad altogether if you ask me. He hasn't even had a proper education, did you know that? He is as thick as too short planks. All he knows about is the armed forces," Arie retorted. "Adriaan what do you think?"

"It looks dangerous, but the worst thing at the moment is the Jewish problem. Yesterday even Hungary adopted the anti-Jewish law. They might have to expel 300,000 of them. Where will they all go?" His educated voice sounded concerned when he added, "What if the Nazis would get a hold in this country, would our Jews be persecuted, would we allow them to do that?"

"No, never. Christ, that doesn't bear thinking about, does it. We'll have to wait and see and hope for the best," my father concluded.

Then it was the turn of the football. Adriaan did not participate, he changed his attention to the older nieces and nephews and the women, who talked about the kids, cooking, the athletic club and everything else they could think of, but not about war, politics or football.

*   *   *   *

38

On Monday August 28th Holland mobilised its troops. Queen Wilhelmina announced over the radio, "I confirm this on the assumption and trust that none of the fighting parties would want to involve the Netherlands in the war. But we must now keep a cool head and do our duties cheerfully and conscientiously." A similar message was broadcast from the government.

On September 1st my father came running in the door.

"Mien, have you heard, the Germans have invaded Poland. Now there will be trouble. England and France have a pact to help them. They're not going to stand for that and that's for sure. They've got to do something. I'm sure those two big countries will soon sort those bastards out."

On September 3rd England and France declared war on Germany. The Dutch nation was in shock and frightened.

3

Overrun

Life in our small community carried on as normal. However, the war was the topic of every conversation. People talked of storing food and building air-raid shelters. Mothers started to worry about their young sons, and young wives about their husbands. When my father was home he spent most of the time glued to the radio listening to every scrap of news.

When all military leave was cancelled on November 12th 1939, everybody waited for the inevitable. Rumours went round that the Germans would invade that same day. As a defence against the invasion various parts of the country were being flooded, meaning that a vast amount of people had to leave their homes.

When nothing happened everybody relaxed a little and Saint Nicholas' Eve on December 5th and Christmas were celebrated in relative calm.

Churches at Christmas were fuller then ever in the vain hope that a trip to the House of God, and prayer, would ward off what was about to happen.

Wishing each other a happy New Year at the party in my grandparents' home must have been hard as the future was bleak, but the belief that Holland could stay neutral was still a remote possibility and people were holding on to this belief even though they knew in their hearts that their hopes were in vain.

On January 10th 1940 both my parents were listening to the radio.

"Christ, Mien, did you hear that, they've shot down a Messerschmitt in Mechelen, that's just south of Antwerp, and they've found plans to invade Belgium, Luxembourg and part of Holland."

"Yes, dear, I'm not deaf, I'm listening to the radio as well."

"Hang on, General Reynders is saying it's part of a nerve war and shouldn't be taken seriously. What's the matter with the stupid man? The Krauts are not just sitting there drawing up plans for fun, are they?"

"No, wouldn't have thought so, but then you never know what those idiots are going to do next, do you? Anyway, parliament still believes we can stay neutral and I'm sure they know what they're talking about."

"I hope they do, but I'm beginning to wonder. I'll tell you those plans weren't made for nothing and that's for sure. Parliament is just trying to keep the nation from panicking, that's what I think anyway."

"You're probably right but it's no good worrying about it at the moment is it? We'll have to wait and see."

The roles were quite reversed now. It was my father who did the worrying and my mother was back to her normal optimistic self after my birth. She was now the one who tried to reassure him and keep his spirits up. She managed to do this all through the war and only very occasionally did I see her cry when it all became too much for her, mainly when there was no food to feed us.

This Messerschmitt saga was still a matter of discussion sixteen days later at the party to celebrate my first birthday.

Spring was approaching and the nice weather cheered people up somewhat. My mother quite often took me for a walk in the park, which was not very far from our house.

I started to walk when I was about eleven months. It became apparent that there was something not quite right with my left foot. It turned in and I kept falling over my own feet. My mother was forever telling me to put my foot straight but I was too small to understand what she meant and even if I had understood there was nothing I could do about it.

To go to the park we had to walk to the end of our road 'under the dyke', climb the concrete steps and then walk 'on top of the dyke' past the windmill, to the park. The park was at the end of a very posh estate and when you lived there you had really made it in life. The houses facing the main road were large to our standards and had big windows and very neat front gardens. Some of Uncle Adriaan's friends lived on that estate.

It was a long way for my little legs but my mother thought it was a good exercise and she would try very hard to make me walk properly.

"Put that little foot straight, you'll fall over otherwise. Now up the steps, lift your foot and put it straight on the next step. Good girl."

However hard I tried I couldn't do it properly, and let loose to run in the park I would trip myself up as my left foot got constantly in the way of the right one. It was rather exhausting for me and my mother always carried me on the way home. We didn't have pushchairs in those days, or at least our family didn't, and when you had grown out of the big pram you were either carried or you had to walk. When going out on the bicycles I would sit in a little chair that hung from the handlebars and later when I had outgrown that in a little seat on the back.

In the end my mother took me to the doctor and he prescribed walking with my bare feet in the sand and arch supports in my little shoes to keep my toes pointing in the right direction. Luckily this treatment worked and I could walk properly before I was four.

On April 19th Prime Minister de Geer proclaimed a state of siege for the whole country. It sent another shock wave through the nation. People panicked, suitcases were being packed just in case we had to flee. God knows where to and how, as the only transport we possessed were bikes, but maybe it made people feel that they were prepared for everything.

We lived in a very vulnerable part of Holland with Rotterdam and Hook of Holland close by and right on the most important river in the kingdom.

Two days later, however, most of those in the country, or at least all the football fans, were in a different state of excitement. The big match between Belgium, their arch rivals in football, and Holland was on in Amsterdam. My father was again glued to the radio. When a goal was scored he cheered very loudly but when something went wrong he cursed and swore at the top of his voice. We all had to be very quiet so he wouldn't miss anything of the commentary. The result 4-2 for Holland brought a lot of the men to the bridge in Maassluis where the whole match was being analysed.

"Brilliant, brilliant, what a match, wished I could have been there," my father kept telling everybody who wanted or didn't want to listen. For a few hours the war had been relegated to second place and over-excitement had taken hold of an enormous part of the population. I wonder what it was like for the poor Belgians who were just as worried about a possible war as the Dutch.

I loved going shopping with my mother. She would dress me up in my little white coat and matching bonnet which she had knitted, and carry me to the shops to save my little legs for the way home when I had to walk holding her one hand while she carried the heavy bag with her other.

I was always allowed to sit on the counter in the co-op where the groceries were bought. If I behaved they gave me a biscuit. In the butcher's a piece of sausage. These shopping trips could take ages because my mum knew so many people and they all wanted to talk to her.

"Hello Mien, hello Willy, little darling. Everything OK? How's Kardien? Worried I bet, like my Pete. Talks about nothing else than the Germans."

"Yes, that's just like Kardien, glued to the radio all the time he's at home. When friends come round they talk about nothing else. Drives me mad. Are you stocking any food, Louise? I can't afford to buy anything extra I'm afraid so that's simple, but they do say everything will be in short supply if we're drawn into this war. I hope to God we can stay out of it. What do you really think,

Louise, will we start fighting?"

"Oh, I don't know really, I'm trying not to think about it. Putting your head in the sand, really, but it's the only way to stay sane, we'll have to wait and see. Oh, by the way, they had some nice wool in the sale in the shop in the New Street. Got some just in case."

I had been pulling my mother's hand impatiently, because she'd promised we would pop into my grandmother's if we had enough time.

"Stop pulling, for Heaven's sake child."

"Want Grandma."

"Yes, OK, we will go to grandma. Cheap wool, did you say, really? I'll go and have a look myself then. You can never have enough wool I always say. Anyway, must carry on. Little madam is getting impatient."

"See you, Mien, bye Willy."

"See you Louise, give my love to Pete."

Conversations like that were the order of the day. The looming war was uppermost in everybody's mind.

I loved going to my grandma and Aunt Bep, who was unmarried and lived at home. She would make me hot chocolate and there were mostly nice biscuits. My grandpa and grandma, who were sitting opposite each other at the table, seemed always pleased to see us. Grandpa had worked until he was really old and was now enjoying a well-deserved rest. Aunt Bep did most of the housekeeping and cooking and made sure that the clothes of Adriaan and Jo were always clean and ironed. Grandma did all the easy jobs like mending and peeling the potatoes and vegetables.

Back home Mum would plonk me on the kitchen table so I wasn't in her way in the tiny kitchen.

"Sit still, so you don't fall off, and leave the shopping alone while I put things away."

When she wasn't looking I would search until I'd find the butter, packed in greaseproof paper. I would wriggle my finger inside the loosely packed parcel, stick my finger in deep, pull it out carefully and lick it off. To this day I've never tasted anything

44

nicer than this lick of freshly churned, slightly salted butter, which was scooped out of a barrel.

"You little tike, what did I tell you, leave the shopping alone." A hard smack on my hand was the result but I would do exactly the same thing whenever I had the chance.

On May 4th the whole family gathered once again for my grandmother's birthday. It was to be the last one in peace for five long years. Six days later, on May 10th 1940, the Germans marched into Holland. We were paralysed with fright. Three of my mother's brothers were somewhere at sea and nobody knew what had happened to them.

Aeroplanes came over our town in the very early hours of the morning. A few people went to the 'Head' and saw them coming over very low. What they didn't see, however, was that they were dropping mines into the Waterway effectively closing us off from the sea.

Neighbours appeared on the street, hardly dressed at this early hour, woken up by the roar of the aeroplanes, not knowing what was going on. Everybody was talking to everybody. It was as if this dreadful news had made this small community into one large family. They were all frightened but they tried to calm each other's nerves. Some women comforted a near hysterical mother with a son in the army who in her disturbed mind was already dead.

Queen Wilhelmina addressed the population on the radio: "After our country with scrupulous conscientiousness had observed strict neutrality, Germany made a sudden attack on our territory without any warning." She asked the people to take up arms with "utmost vigilance and with that inner calm which comes from a clear conscience."

"They'll drive the bastards out, I bet," said my father. We've got a brilliant army, they'll teach those barbarians a bloody lesson I'll tell you." He probably didn't believe these words himself, but it might have made him feel better.

People went to work as normal, but not a lot was achieved in the way of production. Measures were put into place to cope with all sorts of disasters.

"Jan and I have volunteered for the factory's fire brigade," announced my father when he came home. "We'll have to have a bit of training, of course, but the bosses have been very quick getting things organised."

Jan, who was my father's older brother, also worked in the carpet factory.

The very next day the first disaster happened. A mine, which had only been laid the day before, sank a pilot boat carrying the Dutch gold reserves from Rotterdam to London. It happened very close to our town. Maassluis had lost the first ten men in this awful, useless war.

All the anguish was lost on me being still so small but I did find it odd that my sister and I had to go to bed with all our clothes on. Suitcases were also at the ready. Bedtime stories seemed to have disappeared. I found it all rather strange and when my father listened to the radio with a distorted face, which really frightened me, I would hide under the table. Friends, who were always popping in, were not the jolly people I knew. They hardly said hello to me and even my sister seemed to have changed.

The Germans had planned to imprison our whole Royal Family and the Government but they failed and with the help of the English, Princess Juliana, her husband Prince Bernhard and their two young daughters, Beatrix and Irene were safely brought to England on the English vessel *Codrington*. Juliana and the girls went on to Canada but Bernhard stayed in London and assisted his mother-in-law all through the war years.

The next day, on May 13th, Queen Wilhelmina sailed from Hook of Holland to Harwich on the English ship *Hereward*. A few days later the whole Dutch government also arrived in England. At least our Royal Family was safe and the Germans had been thwarted.

"Well, Mien, it seems to be a fact now. The Queen and parliament have gone to England. Sounds like they're fleeing, but if they stayed here they would probably be killed. At least they can work together with the English over there."

"Don't give up hope, our soldiers are still fighting, you said yourself they've shot a few German planes down."

"No love, they're being wiped out, you have to face the truth."

On May 14th, a beautiful, sunny day, Rotterdam was bombed. Within a few minutes the German Heinkels destroyed nearly 25,000 houses, 2,500 shops and hundreds of factories. Rotterdam had lost its heart. The whole of the centre was flattened. Hundreds of people were killed and thousands more made homeless. The battle was lost.

Our soldiers had fought bravely but they were no match for the Blitzkrieg of the Germans. Many soldiers and ordinary people had lost their lives in those first few days.

The next day our tiny country was forced to capitulate, after being threatened that Amsterdam and The Hague would suffer the same fate as Rotterdam if we did not lay down our arms. The islands on the south-west coast, which is the province of Zeeland, still fought on but they too were forced to surrender three days later. Many soldiers were made prisoners of war and died in concentration camps.

On May 29th Arthur Seyss-Inquart, an Austrian lawyer, was installed as Reichskommissar (commissioner) of the occupied Netherlands. For five years he was our cruel ruler.

A few days later my mother's sister, Aunt Dit, came to visit. She had cycled from the neighbouring town of Vlaardingen where she lived with her husband Ger and her little daughter Corrie.

Nothing made my mother happier then being with her sister. They would sit cosily at the table in the small, neat living-room, cups of coffee in front of them. At such occasions I was allowed to sit on top of the table with the large box of buttons, which I used to play 'shop' with. This was always a sign that I had to be quiet.

"I've got news from our brothers Gerrit and Tienus," she said.

"Oh, brilliant, what exactly happened?" my mother asked anxiously.

"Well, according to mother, the trawler which Gerrit is sailing on was on its way from IJmuiden to England when the news of the invasion came through. They just carried on and will stay in England and offer their services to the English Navy.

"Good God, wonder what Riek and the children must be thinking. I do feel for them. Let's just hope Gerrit will be safe. You know what our brothers are like, the bigger the adventure the better. What about Tienus?"

My Uncle Tienus was my mother's dearest and most loved brother, probably because he was the youngest of her real siblings. He was married and lived quite close to us. His marriage was not very happy and when things went badly wrong he would stay in our house for a few days. We saw a lot of him. He sailed on a trawler and he would often bring us fresh fish straight from the boat.

"Tienus was on his way back from England, but when the news came through, they turned round and they will also be volunteering for the English Navy."

"That's three of them then."

"Why, who's the third?"

"Well Dirk, of course. The Smit & Co's tug he's sailing on at the moment was stationed in Vlissingen. As soon as the trouble started they sailed to England, also to help the English."

"Good Lord, I didn't know that. How's Lien taking it?"

"She seemed OK yesterday, but you know what she's like, she moans even if nothing is wrong."

"Yes, that family of hers are a right bunch of smilers. I don't even ask how they are any more because the answer is always the same, 'not very well, had this and that.' They feel ill when a fart sits sideways." Roaring with laughter they continued to imitate my Aunt Lien's family.

They were both excellent at impersonating people and some of our rather eccentric neighbours were often the subjects.

"How's the spy?" asked my aunt.

"In shock I think. She didn't see the Germans coming in her little mirror. Poor old soul, I do feel sorry for her. That son of hers is not a lot of help either; he's as gloomy as the day is long. Problem is every time I'm coming home from somewhere she's at the door. One of these days I'll turn the bloody mirror round."

In those days many people had small mirrors fastened at rectangles to the outside of the windows. They would sit behind their net curtains and spy on everything. The little mirrors were

My Mum and Dad (Kardien and Wilhelmina) on their
wedding day in September 1929.

Me in the park in Vlaardingen, holding my
green knitted rabbit 'Kees'.

My mum, aunt Dit and her daughter Corrie
– I am in the pram.

Mum, Dad, my sister Dicky and me.

Me with my cousin Corrie in the Park in Vlaardingen.

Captain Eerde van Teylingen, my mother's father.

Mum and Dad, my father's brother Jo (left) and my mother's
brother Tienus (right) on the beach in Hook of Holland
long before the war.

called 'little spies', hence the nickname for our neighbour.

After having gone through all the neighbours and the usual questions about each other's families it was time for her to depart.

"Better go now Mien, because I have to fetch Corrie. With all those Germans about now I won't let her walk on her own from school. After all, she's only six. I already found cycling over here frightening. They're bloody everywhere. They didn't do anything but you feel sort of intimidated. Anyway, we'll have to make the best of it. Why don't you cycle over on Sunday when it's nice, maybe we can take the kids to the park."

"Might just do that now it's still possible. Will get Kardien away from the radio for a change. Give Corrie a big kiss and love to Ger. How is he nowadays?"

"Oh, he's still the same, still drinking too much. Anyway, maybe the beer will run out. That would be a good thing at least. Would serve the bugger right. Bye Willy, darling, maybe see you on Sunday and we can go and see the little deer in the park."

"Bye Auntie."

A big hug followed and off she went.

Hundreds of families had suddenly lost husbands and fathers as trawlers, coasters, tugs and various other vessels had sailed for England. For five whole years they never saw their men and only occasionally did they get news. Many of them never returned.

Life went back to some form of normality even though the place was crawling with arrogant, self-assured Germans. People were forced to take Germans into their houses or were thrown out altogether for them to occupy. All trawlers, tug boats and pilot boats in the outer harbour had been replaced by German ships. The resistance started sabotaging telephone and electricity supplies, trying hard to frustrate the Germans. I don't think my father was ever really involved but he knew all about it.

Holland was in turmoil but convinced that the war wouldn't last long because England, that mighty country, was our friend and ally. They would soon come to our aid and beat the Germans back to their own country.

c

Rationing was quickly introduced.

"Mien, I've just heard that tea and coffee are going to be rationed," said our neighbour Marie.

"What? Why is that?"

"I don't know but I suppose they can't get things shipped in now. I'm going to get a few packs in the Co-op and maybe Mol has got some."

Mol was the owner of the little shop on the corner of our street.

"Better go and tell Mother and Bep, so they can go and get some, they use so much with all the visitors they get. God, whatever will be next. Anyway maybe it's just a rumour. Still better go and tell them. Thanks Marie, for letting me know."

On the first of June 1940 tea and coffee were rationed and bread and flower followed on the 15th. Textiles were next on August 12th and meat on September 14th. Things were getting tough.

My father, quite an impatient man at times, became more and more frustrated. His language deteriorated by the day and as I was just learning to talk I found all those words highly interesting.

"Mum, she's doing it again," my sister would inform my mother.

"She's sitting under the table using every swear word she can think of."

"Yes, I know, just leave her. If I tell her off she will do it even more."

"Stupid kid, you're disgusting," my sister muttered. "I'll tell Dad about you."

Totally oblivious of her disgust I carried on happily spouting my 'bloody hells', 'bastards', 'shit bags' and whatever else I had picked up.

Hundreds of years earlier Holland had been in the same grip of fear. From the early 1300s the Low Countries were ruled by France but when in 1516 Duke Charles of Burgundy, who was also Archduke of Austria and Holy Roman Emperor, became King of Spain we were automatically put under Spanish control.

Charles tried to stop the spread of the Reformation, which was sweeping our part of the country, by prosecuting the Calvinists (Protestants), however, his actions brought little success. His son, Philip II, inherited the Low Countries in 1555 and he decided to step up the fight against the Reformation. He appointed Margaret of Austria, Duchess of Parma as the governor-general of the Netherlands to strengthen and increase the pressure.

In 1566 a group of Calvinists petitioned Margaret to relax the religious persecution of the Protestants. They were partially successful and they had no objection, therefore, that she gave them the nickname Geuzen (beggars).

Philip was not satisfied with the way Margaret dealt with the Calvinists and at the end of 1567 decided to replace her with the Duke of Alva. He was known for his tyranny and from the start initiated a reign of terror. He set up the Council of Troubles, nicknamed the Council of Blood. He set aside all local laws and condemned, dispossessed and executed thousands of people.

In 1568 the Low Countries revolted and that was the start of the Eighty-year War. William I of Orange (William the Silent), who had been appointed Stadtholder of Holland, Zeeland and Utrecht, led the revolt and fought bravely but because of a lack of funds he was doomed to failure.

In the meantime, the Geuzen had grown rapidly. This powerful guerrilla force was drawn from all the Low Countries' provinces but was centred in Holland and Zeeland. They were mainly made up from lesser nobility and magnates. They conducted pillages in the country and raided the Spanish ships at sea.

On April 1st 1572 the Geuzen seized the port of Brielle, which lies on one of the islands west of Rotterdam. This port was of enormous strategic value and Alva was not pleased. He already was a disappointed man because he had not been able to push through heavy taxation and was about to return to Spain, but he was so infuriated by the fall of Brielle that he started a counter-offensive. The southern provinces were soon brought back under control, then towns in the north fell, but resistance was so great that the Spanish army had to give up and Alva returned to Spain in 1573.

The Geuzen had by now complete control of Holland and Zeeland thus securing them against Spanish attacks. They stayed the revolt's main force until 1576 when other provinces joined the resistance and they were replaced by a regular military army. The Spanish never forced their way into Holland again.

In 1579 Holland and six other northern provinces declared its independence from Spain, calling it the United Provinces of the Low Countries (The Netherlands). It took until 1648 before this was recognised by Spain.

Every year the historic event of the seizure of Brielle is re-enacted by the local people. It is quite a spectacle and certainly worth watching.

As soon as the Germans had entered our country a resistance army was formed. The name they chose for their organisation was, not surprisingly, the Geuzen, the old name given to those brave people who fought their oppressor. This time his name was not the Duke of Alva but Adolf Hitler.

The Geuzen movement in Maassluis grew rapidly. They knew they had to be careful, but as this was a totally new experience for everybody involved, they didn't realise just how careful.

They had also no idea of the fact that there were actually people in our town who sympathised with the Germans. It was absolutely inconceivable in the ordinary person's eyes that anybody could be friendly towards the intruders. How wrong they were.

Also their misguided belief was that even if they were caught they would just spend some time in prison. They never envisaged that the consequences could be so devastating. The first time they learned that they had been betrayed by German sympathisers was in December 1940.

Weapons, which had been discovered in a munitions bunker in a different part of the country, were secretly shipped in wooden crates to Maassluis. The lettering on the crates read 'Machine parts for N.V. van Raalt', a large factory in Maassluis. They were then packed in waterproof crates and sunk in the inner harbour. Nobody knew anything about it apart from a very small group of the resistance army. Or so they thought.

On December 2nd Jacques Boezeman, the ringleader, was arrested. The crates were lifted from the harbour bed. Beaten and kicked by German soldiers in full view of other inhabitants he was taken to a prison in Scheveningen. On January 8th 1941 he was brought from his cell to be interrogated by the Sicherheits Dienst (German Security Police) in The Hague. He was tortured and his wrists cut. He never spoke. He died the next morning. He was the first resistance fighter in the country to be murdered by the Germans.

"Kardien, they've murdered Jacques Boezeman," my father was told by one of his colleagues.

"Oh, Jesus, the poor man, what did they do to him?"

"According to stories smuggled out of the prison, they tortured him and he died from his injuries, but he never gave anything away."

"So hopefully all the others are safe. I hope one day they'll find the bastards who betrayed them, then they can give them the same treatment."

The others were not safe, however, because in January and February more were arrested. Many were shot and others sent to Buchenwald. Fear had taken hold of everybody. The Germans had shown their true face. The face of cruelty and power.

The cinema at the end of our road was now only for the Germans. At night the people in our street would stand on their doorsteps and watch them go past with their Dutch girlfriends, who we called 'moffegrieten' or German's trollops. We just stood there, the whole neighbourhood, watching them in silence. It was far too dangerous to make comments because they would shoot you for less.

When my mother saw her brother Tienus's wife come past on the arm of a German she nearly passed out.

One day when my mum and dad were still indoors I had already sneaked outside and when the first couple passed I shouted out in a loud voice, "Mum, the 'ollops are here." My mother must have nearly died on the spot. I got a hard smack and I was dragged indoors. I had no idea what I'd done wrong, but I never said the word out loud again.

If the Dutch people lived in fear, it must have been far worse for the large Jewish population. Slowly but surely they were squeezed out of ordinary life. Already in October 1940 signs were put up in many cafés stating 'Jews are not welcome here'. If they didn't comply, the Germans would close those businesses down or worse arrest the owners. All companies owned by Jews had to register. The ones who were working in the public services could no longer be promoted. They all had to fill in a declaration that they were Jewish. They also had to give the name of their spouse, their parents and grandparents. By November they were sacked from their jobs. Our most well known Jewish family was butcher van Gelderen who had a thriving business in the market square.

"Do you still buy your meat from van Gelderen, Mien?" asked my father.

"Yes, of course, even more now then ever, that is to say what meagre rations I can get with the coupons."

"Wonder if he had to register his business, poor sod. Has always worked hard, lived here all his live, doing nobody any harm. It makes you feel so useless, so bloody frustrated. What have they ever done to those sodding Krauts? They have that lovely daughter, too. Oh, God if only there was anything we could do."

But there was very little anybody could do unless you had room in your house somewhere where you could hide people or live in the countryside where thousands were hidden. Later in the war this family was taken away by the Germans never to be seen again.

4

Shortages

Listening to the radio became a hazardous business. The Germans were now, of course, in control of all the radio stations. Dutch stations could still broadcast but they were not allowed to say anything negative about our oppressors or the war in general.

From the beginning of July 1940 it was an offence to listen to foreign stations. If caught you would either be severely punished or maybe even sent to a concentration camp.

Already by the end of July a Dutch radio station, called Radio Oranje, had been set up in London and was broadcast by the BBC. Allowed or not everybody with a good radio listened to it. Mind you the volume had to be turned right down for fear of the Germans hearing it. When, much later in April 1943, all radios had to be handed in and possessing one became illegal, my father hid his in the ceiling and listened with headphones to those vital bulletins.

When something important had happened my father would write it on a piece of paper, pin it with a safety pin to my vest and I was then taken by him to one of his friends, where the piece of paper was removed, read and destroyed while they talked of everyday things. Later when I was a bit older I was sent on my own, never very far away of course, just to people in the neighbourhood who didn't have the use of a radio.

Nobody dared discuss the war in the street because if you were caught talking about things you were not supposed to know, you could lose your life. They only talked about the war indoors and then only with very close friends and family because nobody could now be trusted.

Food was already getting scarce. However, we were not yet hungry. Vegetables and fruit were still available and so were dairy products. After December 1940 cooking had to be done at certain times because even gas and electricity had by then been rationed.

Lots of things were just not there any more or only available in very small quantities and you had to have the correct coupons. This was the case one day with the lard. My Aunty Dit had come for the day and she had managed to get some fish for lunch.

We always ate our hot meal at lunch-time, when my father had his lunch break and my sister came home from school at twelve before returning at two. My mother was delighted with the lovely fresh fish but when she looked for something to fry it in her face dropped.

"Blast, I haven't got any fat left and I can't get any more either because I've used up all my coupons. Now what are we going to do?"

"Can't you steam it?" suggested my aunt.

"Yes, I could but that's not very nice with this sort of fish, is it?"

"No, I suppose not, but it's better than nothing."

"Hang on," said my mother, "I wonder if the little spy next door has some dripping in her meat-safe. She's so blooming mean, she never runs out of anything. She saves every little spoonful of fat and keeps tipping it in a bowl."

"Will she give you some, when you ask?" said my aunt.

"Give me some; are you joking? She would rather die. No we'll have to pinch a bit."

"Pinch it, you must be mad. Where is that meat-safe anyway?"

"On the outside wall in her backyard, I'm sure I can reach it with the stepladder. It's only just on the other side of the fence. I looked in it the other day when I was cleaning the back windows and I saw a big bowl full."

"Hasn't she got spy-mirrors on her back window?"

"No, you idiot, of course not. Now are we going to do it or not?"

"Oh, Mien I don't know, what if she catches us out?"

"Well we cross that bridge when we get to it. Come on, don't be such a coward."

"Oh, all right then, let's give it a go."

I was, of course, told to stay indoors and keep quiet, but at least I could follow the proceedings from the back window.

The stepladder was very carefully taken from the shed and put as close as possible near to the wooden fence which divided our yards. Because they had to do everything as quietly as they could they were both getting the giggles. My aunt was holding the stepladder while my mother first looked if anybody was about and then very carefully unhooked the latch and opened the mesh door of the small meat-safe. 'Peeeeeeeep' went the door.

My aunt was shaking so much with suppressed laughter that it made my mother wobble precariously on top of the ladder.

"Stop it, for God's sake, I'm nearly falling off," she whispered.

With the utmost care the bowl of dripping was lifted out and handed to my aunt. 'Peeeeeep' went the door again when my mother shut it. By the time they were back in the kitchen they were both falling about laughing and I kept hearing them going 'peeeep'.

"God, I hope she's deaf," said my aunt.

"No, she's not, but let's hope she's too busy spying what's going on in the street. Now let's get some of this stuff. A big spoonful should be enough. No, what I'll do is to take two, melt them down, pour some of it over the top of the bowl and nobody will be any the wiser."

The peeeeep was heard twice more when the bowl was replaced.

As soon as my dad came home, he knew those two had been up to something by the looks on their faces. When they told him the story he could hardly believe that they had dared to do anything like that.

"You cheeky buggers, what would you have done if you'd been caught?"

"I don't know, honestly I don't, but anyway we got away with it, so just enjoy your fish," said my mum.

I'm sure that fish tasted better than anything else we had ever eaten.

It was always fun when my aunt was there but this particular lunch-time was quite hilarious. Every time those two looked at each other they went 'peeeeeeep' and a fresh salvo of laughter erupted. Of course, the story was related to my grandparents and Aunt Bep, who all thought it was very naughty but funny nevertheless.

Fish was never my favourite dish and I mostly ate it under protest. I drew the line, however, at smoked eel. At that time in the war this was still available and very cheap but just the look of those long horrid things made me heave. I would not eat it. One day at lunch I found it very strange that my mother had mashed up my food for me. I knew something was odd. The others were having those dreaded eel things.

"I don't like eels," I protested.

"No, darling, you're having chicken, Mummy has mixed it up with your food."

Poking through it, all I could see was some whitish meat, so I believed her and I ate every scrap on my plate, it was so nice.

"Did you like the chicken?" asked my mum afterwards.

"Yes, Mummy, it was 'licious."

"Well, it wasn't chicken, it was smoked eel, so now you know that you do like it."

I felt betrayed and quite upset that my mum had lied to me but couldn't deny the fact that it was lovely. Until this day it is my most favourite food, but it is now, even in Holland, a very expensive delicacy.

My mother was very good with her hands. She could knit, sew, embroider, darn, mend and everything else that was required of a good housewife in those days. Clothes for my sister and me and for herself were mostly homemade. But textiles were rationed now and there was very little in the shops. She was, therefore, delighted when she managed to get some parachute linen. It was immediately taken to show Aunt Bep.

"Gosh, Mien, that's lovely. Where did you get it from?"

"From Marie next door, don't ask me how she got it, but you know what she's like, she never sews anything for her four kids, so she really didn't know what to do with it. I have a feeling one of her relations in The Hague got hold of it. I paid for it mind, I thought that was only fair. I'm going to make a blouse for Dicky out of it first and hopefully one for myself. I want to put elastic in the sleeves instead of a cuff, that seems to be more fashionable these days. I just hope I can get some. I'm going to have a look now."

"Have you got enough sewing thread?"

"I think so, but I might be able to get some more."

Grandma also thought it was lovely and promised to help out with the thread if there wasn't any available.

We set off for the haberdashery in the New Street straight away.

"Can I help you?" said the lady when we entered the near empty shop.

"Yes, I wonder if you've got any elastic?" my mum said, dreading the answer would be no.

"You're lucky we've got some in because it's hard to come by nowadays. We really have to ration it and a metre is all we can let you have I'm afraid."

"Well, it will have to do. I'm hoping to make two blouses with elastic in the sleeves, so it should be all right. I'm just grateful you've got some."

"Quite, because it's becoming more and more difficult to get anything at all. It's no fun any more in the shop, I can assure you."

"No, I can understand that."

She also managed to get a reel of cotton, so all was set for the sewing party. My mother must have been in a hurry because she carried me both ways. On our way home she still found time to pop into Grandma's again just to tell her she'd managed to get what she wanted.

59

Back home the dining table was cleared and out came the brown paper. A large sheet with umpteen patterns on it was placed on top of the paper and the funny little tool, which makes small holes in the pattern and on the paper underneath it, was used to trace the lines. The pattern was quickly cut out and put on the material.

"Get out the way a bit Willy, go and play with your bricks or your doll. I'm using pins and I don't want you to get hurt. I want to get this basted before Dicky comes home lunch-time, so she can fit it."

"I want to watch," I said still perched on one of the chairs overlooking the table.

"Well you can't. When Mummy gets the sewing machine out this afternoon, you can sit on the table and play shop with the buttons. Go and get an apple and be quiet."

I wasn't very happy but did as I was told.

After dinner when my father had gone back to work and, in my eyes, my stupid sister, who I blamed for the discomfort in the morning, had gone back to school the Singer sewing machine was at last placed on the table.

"Now don't touch anything, but play with the buttons."

"Yes Mummy."

I used to play for hours with the buttons, there must have been at least two hundred of them, in all colours and sizes. I would sort them by colour, put them in heaps and that was my ware.

"What would you like, madam? Oh, peas, yes here you are. That is three cents, please." Sometimes I had bits of paper, so I could wrap the merchandise up. I loved it, but after a while I got a bit bored. I watched my mother's hand furiously turning the sewing machine handle, totally engrossed in her work. It was then that I spotted the elastic.

I had heard in the shop that it was difficult to come by, so surely my customers would like some too.

"Would you like some 'lastic, madam?" I whispered to my imaginary customer.

Carefully I grabbed the scissors and cut a piece for my client.

"You want some as well? Yes fine, but you can only have little bits you know because I do not have very much."

And that was precisely what my customers got. I doled out tiny pieces until none was left. Then my mother noticed.

I knew by the look on her face that I had done something very wrong. I got lifted off the table, got my bottom smacked hard and really shouted at and that didn't happen very often. I cried my little eyes out but there was no mercy. No cuddle to soothe my pain. For the first time in my life I was well and truly in the doghouse.

My sister was so mad with me she didn't speak to me for two days. The blouses were eventually finished, but without elastic.

Life for me was happy though, still hardly understanding what was going on. My father's pale blue eyes looked often grim and he would talk to my mother in the kitchen or he had whispered conversations at night with his friends. It seemed to me that people didn't talk out loud any more. I did not understand that for them the walls had ears and traitors were around everywhere.

There were quite a few NSB people in our town and they were even worse than the Germans (Members of the National Socialist Party or Dutch Nazis).

Some of the people in the neighbourhood had sons who were in camps, imprisoned after we capitulated. Nothing was heard from them and nobody knew if they were dead or alive. When my mother met the parents she would always ask if they'd heard anything, but the answer was always the same. In the end she just stopped asking.

Little bits of news came from my mother's three brothers. We didn't know at the time if they were sailing on English or Dutch vessels or where they were, but at least if some news trickled through we knew they were alive.

In the early days of May 1940 a large part of the Royal Dutch Navy had managed to escape to England and about 6000 officers and ratings were now fighting with the allies, sailing under the Dutch flag. Even the Royal Marine Institute, which was based in Den Helder, in the North of Holland, had been transported to Cornwall so that about sixty naval cadets could finish their training.

The exiled Dutch government did their utmost best to strengthen the fleet and half of the available funds were spent on the Navy. Even a half finished destroyer, the *Isaac Sweers* and a light cruiser, the *Jacob van Heemskerck*, had been towed over to be finished at English shipyards.

After having fought very bravely the *Isaac Sweers* was torpedoed on November 13th 1942. Only about eighty of the two hundred men survived.

Our mine-sweepers helped the English clear mines to keep vital supply routes open.

More than eight hundred other vessels, freighters, coasters, tugs and liners took part in the war all around the world. Trawlers were used for fishing in the Irish Sea. Nearly five hundred of those vessels never returned, with the loss of numerous lives.

We had no way of knowing if those three brothers were still on their own ships or where they were but it didn't make any difference because they were fighting our common enemy.

My mother was very proud that three of her siblings were actually taking part in the action and she would often talk about it with friends and family. She was worried about them, of course, but when news arrived that they were safe and sound she would run to my grandparents and tell them the good tidings.

Birthdays in Holland are always celebrated in grand style and all the friends and family, including the children, come to the party at night. It became difficult to do this, not only because of the shortages but because the curfew in the coastal areas was from 10pm until 4am, while the rest of the country had to stay in between midnight and 4am.

A massive defence line had been built on the western coastline of Holland, and Maassluis formed part of that. Enormous concrete barricades had been built on the approach roads to our small town and the German Navy occupied the outer harbour.

We could still travel on the train and journeys to Vlaardingen, where some of my father's relations and my mother's sister lived, were quite frequently undertaken if the weather did not permit us to go by bike.

If, however, life for the ordinary people in Holland became more and more frustrating it really was nothing compared to what the Jewish population was then suffering.

One day in the latter part of February 1941 my father was looking particularly gloomy. News had filtered through of the first razzia in Amsterdam whereby four hundred young Jewish men had been rounded up. They were transported to Mauthausen, a camp in Germany, and never seen again. Massive strikes were organised in many parts of the country to protest against the razzia.

"You know I told you about the strikes after the razzia in Amsterdam, Mien," he said to my mother. "You know what those SS (Schutzstaffel – protection forces) bastards did. They drove through Amsterdam and just shot at anybody they fancied and threw bloody hand grenades. They killed nine people and a lot more were wounded. That's what the rumours are anyway."

"You know, I don't know how people can do that, just shoot innocent people. I mean the people who were on strike weren't killing any Germans, were they, so why would they retaliate like that?" asked my mother.

"It's a game to them, Mien, a show of power. We're nothing to them, just cattle. Well not as bad as the poor Jews I suppose, they really are treated like animals; they're even being transported in cattle trains. Poor sods. God, if only we could do something." A few more choice words would be shouted out in frustration but there was nothing he could do to change the situation.

After the strikes three communists and fifteen resistance people were arrested. They were blamed for the strikes and shot dead without exception on March 13th 1941. In June of the same year more round-ups of Jews followed in Amsterdam and The Hague.

It was now forbidden for them to appear in seaside resorts, parks, cinemas and cafés. Jews who owned their own companies were no longer allowed to manage them. Outsiders were brought in to do that. They no longer had a say in the running of their business, which they had often built up from scratch by pure hard

63

work.

Orchestras were forbidden to employ Jews. This was a further step up from the fact that Jewish musicians had to sit at the back of the orchestra.

In March all Dutch radio station were abolished and all the radio broadcasts were now just German propaganda. The Dutch Nation had also lost its democracy. In June all political parties were forbidden, ninety members of parliament were arrested and jailed.

More Jews were picked up in Amsterdam and deported. In September the first of them died in the gas chambers in Auschwitz. The German boot was getting larger and heavier.

On October 3rd Rotterdam was burning once more. It was May 14th 1940 all over again. People in our street gazed towards the coloured sky but they were not cross or afraid. This time the English were the culprits and we knew that their bombardment was not meant to harm us but to destroy the Germans. More than one hundred people were killed but we realised that we'd not been forgotten and that help would come in the end.

Attentively listening to Radio Oranje on December 7th 1941 my father nearly jumped out of his skin.

"Mien, come here and listen, the Japanese have attacked Pearl Harbour in Hawaii. The Americans will have to join the war now."

"Why, what's Hawaii got to do with America?"

"It's an American base. Ssh, I can't hear clearly. Good God, Japan has declared war on the United States, England, Canada and Australia. Right, I'm going out for a while."

Conversations like this where always whispered and not just because the Germans or their Dutch lackeys were nearly living in your back yard. They were also worried that I might pick up things and blurt them out. After the incident with the 'ollops' they became very careful of what was said or discussed in front of me. I knew, from the strange way they behaved, that what was being said was very important and not meant for my ears, but even if I had been able to hear what they were saying it would have just been gobbledegook to me.

The next day the Dutch Government in London declared war on Japan.

We had drifted into December and had celebrated Saint Nicholas' Eve on December 5th once more. Presents were now hard to come by but my mother had managed somehow to get a few small things for my sister and me. New Year's Eve was again celebrated at home. The curfew had put a stop to celebrating this event in my grandmother's house.

The Dutch people are extremely resilient and will grab every opportunity to show this. To demonstrate to the oppressor that spirits were still unbroken the ice-skating event, the 'Elfstedentocht' (eleven town journey), was held on January 22nd 1942.

This is a national event held in the province of Friesland in the North of Holland. It is not held every year because the ice on all the canals through the eleven towns has to be thick enough to hold an enormous amount of people. The 'ice-master' is responsible for measuring the thickness of the ice and giving the go-ahead.

That year an astonishing 970 competitors were taking part plus nearly 4000 others who took the trip at a leisurely pace. Never before had so many people taken part in this event.

It was extremely cold. In some places the temperature had dropped to minus 27 degrees Celsius, the coldest ever measured in Holland. But they didn't mind the cold and it became a fantastic show of nationalism and defiance.

Most Dutch people love skating and my parents and the rest of the family were no exceptions. Before the war they would skate with the whole family in one long row, holding on to the waist of the person in front, all the way to Vlaardingen. They would go for coffee to either Aunt Truus or my father's brother, Uncle Henk and then skate all the way back again.

Aunt Alida would always be right at the back of the line because she couldn't skate very well, so the rest of them just dragged her along. They wore wooden skates in those days, which were fastened to their ordinary shoes by strong leather or canvas straps. The fancy metal ones were only for rich people and I never had skates with boots attached until I was eighteen.

This winter a lot of people took advantage of the weather and the canals were full of adults and children. It was a superb outlet for their frustrations and they looked happy and relaxed. I was too small, of course, but my parents and my sister spent most of their free time on the ice.

One Sunday afternoon my mother took my sister with her and my dad had to look after me and would take me later to watch them. My father didn't have a clue how to dress me and when we arrived at the canal my mother took one look at me and dissolved into laughter. My little bonnet, which had ribbon threaded through the bottom and tied under my chin, was now perching upside down on my head. The ribbon now framing, or rather obscuring, my face. Where he had tied the ribbon the whole thing had fallen over my face and I was invisible from my nose upwards. He never improved; we always said he had two left hands.

That winter the Dutch population showed the Germans that they could still enjoy themselves. We were not yet completely beaten. We did not have a lot of food but were not yet hungry and the fires in the houses were still burning.

Coalman Paalvast, who was a friend of my parents, was still delivering coal with his horse and cart. I used to love that because he would lift me on top of the horse and I would be allowed to ride on it a little way along the road. The milkman, Jacob van Balen, still delivered the milk every day with the big milk churns loaded on his handcart. Soon life would be back to normal. We were just waiting for the English to come and set us free. The general belief was still that it wouldn't be long now . . .

5

Flag Parade

In times of trouble people change. Friendships are formed but hatred increases. Our neighbourhood had always been a friendly place but now people felt even closer to each other than ever before. On the other hand one or two people were thought to be corroborating with the Germans and they were now cut dead in the street or just greeted with a nod of the head.

When we were walking to my grandmother even more neighbours would stop and have a chat. It must have been some sort of release valve to talk about the daily chores or the kids, just normal things as if nothing was wrong.

There was Mrs Terlaak, the wife of the miller who worked in the windmill that stood proudly on top of the dyke. She was quite a bit older than my mum and whenever we saw her, never mind what time of day, her bright pink slip would always hang at least two inches lower than her dress.

She would mostly moan about the shortage of chocolate because she had a very sweet tooth, which was obvious by the state, or rather the lack, of her teeth. Her coarse, grey hair always looked to be in need of a good brush and I remember vividly that she moaned a lot about her husband. Her children had grown up and flown the nest, so maybe her main occupation had become bemoaning her lot and feeling sorry for herself. My mother dreaded being stopped by her because you could never get away.

Mrs Sluyter, who lived opposite Mrs Terlaak, was certainly a penny short of a pound. She was quite a short, ugly woman with short bandy legs. She was always running around like somebody possessed without achieving anything. Her hair was always in a mess and she wore her stockings in constant Nora Batty fashion. She was extremely kind though and always had time to stop for a chat and to say nice things to me.

She already had four children when she announced proudly that she was pregnant again. She was absolutely delighted. My mother congratulated her and with that news we went to see Grandma and Aunt Bep. It must have been big news because it was mentioned as soon as we entered the house. I, of course, had no idea what 'being pregnant' meant.

"Did you know that Mrs Sluyter was pregnant again, Bep?"

"Good Lord, no I didn't know that. Is she pleased?"

"Absolutely over the moon. I can't understand it, who wants to bring a child into the world during a war, certainly not when you've already got four."

"No, you would think they'd be a bit more careful. Still, as long as she is happy, that's the main thing."

"That's true and I suppose you just can't put a stop to everything just because there's a war on. I just hope everything will go all right for her."

The conversation rolled on but Grandma seemed more interested in me and made no comment. Rather difficult when you have borne ten children yourself. She obviously didn't know how to put a stop to it either.

When Mrs Sluyter gave birth to a son, Arend, my mother and most other people in the street managed to get her a small present. My mother, who had knitted a little jumper as a gift, cooed over the 'beautiful' baby. I couldn't understand that at all because I thought he was even uglier than his mother. It was a sign, however, that war or no war life went on and it made a nice change of conversation.

All the people in the small streets where we lived were simple, hard-working, manual labourers. The next block going towards the cinema was a bit more posh. The houses were bigger and had front and back gardens and mostly housed office workers or shop owners.

One of them was a painter and decorator. He was a pleasant man and always stopped and talked until people were warned that he might be friendly with the Germans. Everybody was on his guard and pleasant natters now became polite conversations about the weather.

In the evenings a lot of people from all over town would take a stroll to 'The Head'. The reason was not just to stretch their legs, but also to show the Germans what this small town thought of them.

The outer harbour in Maassluis had been completely transformed and was now full of small German warships such as mine-sweepers, tugs and lighters. Non-German vessels could no longer reach the harbours along the river.

To the west of the town the river was blocked by U-boats and on both sides of the river a lighter had been anchored. A steel net, attached to a massive steel cable, lay at the bottom of the river in the daytime and was raised at night so that the river was completely closed off between Maassluis and Rozenburg and even U-boats could not get through.

At eight o'clock every evening it was 'Flag Parade', when the German flags on the ships were lowered. When the whistle sounded, marking the start of the ceremony, everybody had to stand to attention until the whistle was blown again marking the end of the procedures. Hundreds of people would be wandering around by the harbour until a couple of minutes before the sound of the whistle was due and then they would all disappear in the side streets leaving the quays deserted. They all re-appeared as soon as the ceremony had finished. It was our way of showing our disgust for the German flag and to needle the despised enemy.

A couple of times some youngsters threw the whole performance into disarray because they blew their own whistle before the German one. It so infuriated the Krauts that for a while nobody was allowed in the harbour area at that time of night. They closed it off by letting the barriers down at the level railway crossing at the entrance to the 'Head' and the harbour.

69

Everybody thought that was hilarious. People still came, stood by the barriers laughing and joking, only to swarm on to the quays as soon as the barriers were raised.

The Dutch population loathed the intruders, but fear of them became an even more overwhelming feeling. It became more and more apparent that you could be shot just for being somewhere at the wrong time in the wrong place. Their eyes were everywhere and just going into town or visiting relations became unpleasant. They were intimidating, self-assured, arrogant bastards. The worst was when they marched singing through the town, leather boots stamping the cobblestones. You had to be careful to stand aside otherwise they would have marched straight over you.

They had problems too though, and because all their men were fighting in one place or another their biggest headache was their constant shortage of people to work in their factories, and our men were now taken from their own places of work in order to be transported to Germany and man their machines. It was a frightening business.

My father was one of the many ordered to have a fitness test. When he came home that night from work he looked as pale as a sheet.

"Mien, I've been told I have to have a medical and if I'm declared fit I'll have to go to Germany."

"Oh, God, no, why, why you? What am I going to do? For how long do you have to go?"

"I don't know. We've just been told to have this medical. I don't know any more than that. Why can't those pigs just leave us alone? They rule your country and now they're starting to run our bloody lives."

He was devastated and at his lowest ebb. My mother was crying and my sister just kept very quiet. I cried because my mum was crying and I did understand that my dad might have to go away.

"Can't you say you have a bad back and that you had sciatica a few years ago and were unable to work for several months," suggested my mother.

"Mien, for Christ's sake, you know there's no way you can talk to those arrogant misfits. They are only capable of giving orders. They don't listen and if they did they would say that they can't understand the language. It's just hopeless, I'll have to go and that's the end of the story. The only thing I can do is fake the same pains as I had with the sciatica. Maybe that will help."

"Well, at least take your walking stick and limp."

He had to have this examination in the Register Office that had been quickly turned into some sort of medical centre. During the few days we were waiting for him to be summoned, our normally happy household had turned into one of sadness and despair. My mother's eyes had gone dull and the spring in her step had somehow gone. My grandparents were frightened too, not only for him but also for their other boys.

At last the day arrived. I have no idea how long it took but for my mother it must have seemed hours. Then a grinning Dad returned home. All the pain he had suffered over the months of his illness had come to good use. He had remembered exactly when to scream with pain and he had been dismissed, declared unfit. Maybe it was cowardly, because now another man would have to go, but his family came before heroism.

At that time only the fit were 'chosen' to go and work for the 'Vaterland'. Later they were not so choosy. Razzias were held and everybody who was only slightly able was put on transport to Germany.

That was the time when people started to go into hiding. My father and some of his brothers would disappear for a couple of days. The word razzia would spread like wildfire through the town and everybody who could possibly hide did so.

In my Aunt Bep's bedroom, hidden by her bed, was a trapdoor. Going through there you came into a place which was in between the roof and the ceiling, a sort of a loft really. At least three of my uncles would hide in there. It was an anxious time. When the coast was clear they would come out and have a quick wash and Aunt Bep would feed them. When the Germans would search the house they hardly dared breathe. Luckily they never found this hiding place.

I had, of course, no idea where he had gone and I had long

71

learned not to ask any questions, as the answers were never forthcoming anyway.

It was a petrifying experience when the leather booted bullies would enter your house to look round. They were rude, intimidating and loud. In June 1942 the first large contingent of Dutch forced labourers was sent to Germany.

As already mentioned, if life for the Dutch people was hard due to fear and ever decreasing rations, it was still worse for the Jewish population. Now forced to wear a star on their clothing, massive deportations were in progress.

Many were in hiding. Many were betrayed and sent to their death and the people who had given them shelter were either shot themselves or sent to concentration camps. Some Jews were even lifted from their hospital beds. A massive camp had been set up in Westerbork, in the Northeast of the country, close to the German border. Thousands of them were sent there, most of them only with the clothes they stood up in. Only a handful ever returned. From there a transport to the gas chambers was the most likely outcome.

Resistance workers were being executed by the hundreds, often betrayed by their own countrymen, who were now the lackeys of the Germans. They were terrible people, even more fanatical and ruthless than their masters. It did not diminish the resistance, however, but made them even more determined to do what they could.

In the villages around our town, many a Jew was hidden and pilots from the allied forces, whose planes had been shot down, found hospitality in the farmhouses until they could be smuggled out of the country and back to their units.

In our small town the resistance was still very much in working order but better organised and more secretive than ever. My cousin's fiancé, Wim Mooiman, was one of them. He related the wonderful tale of the transport of some precious weapons to our family but obviously not until the war was over.

The director of the 'Nutsspaarbank' (public savings bank), which was situated on the other side of the town to where I lived, was a keen and very clever resistance worker. Weapons for the

My paternal grandparents – Grandma and Grandad van der Hoek.

My paternal grandparents' house.

Aunt Bep, my father's sister.

My sister and I at the Market in Maassluis.

Aunt Anna Hoftijzer, my grandfather's sister. She was the aunt who gave food to my sister in the hunger winter.

Uncle Tienus, my mother's brother.

My sister and I posing for an official photograph.

Uncle Adriaan, my father's unmarried brother.

Home Guards had been smuggled into the town and were kept in the safe of this bank.

The Home Guards were under the command of Prince Bernhard, who was, as his mother-in-law Queen Wilhelmina, in London. Very few people knew about this cache, but Wim Mooiman was in on the secret.

When you wanted to take money out or put money into this bank, you entered a small enclosure and shut the door behind you, thus your business was conducted in total privacy. As many people went in and out of the bank even in those days, it was an ideal place for secret messages and activities.

One of the cubicles had another door inside which led to the inner sanctum and the boardroom. 'Special customers' were admitted through this door.

Hidden in the bank were sten guns, bazookas and revolvers. Every weapon had an instruction leaflet, which was studied very carefully by the person in charge of that particular weapon, and when he was sure he understood the workings of the gun, other trusted resistance workers had to be taught how to use them. They couldn't practise shooting with them, of course, because that might have given the game away completely.

The lessons in the handling of the weapons were conducted in the boardroom of this well respected bank. It would have been difficult to find a better place to do this as nobody questioned the comings and goings of people.

One day, however, they were tipped off that the Germans might be suspecting something and a raid on the bank became a possibility. The weapons had to be moved quickly, but how? Baker Gaasbeek suggested that they transport them in his delivery handcart and store them temporarily in his warehouse behind the bakery, which was on top of the dyke. One of the bank clerks, a man called Melis, had the keys to the safe where the weapons were hidden.

"You'd never believe this," Wim recalled, "but on the day of the switch Melis opened the safe, went inside and the door fell shut behind him, so he, the keys and the weapons were locked in. Panic! Luckily the director had a spare set and all was saved."

73

d

The cache was loaded into the bread cart, covered over and a pile of fresh loaves put on top. The lid of the cart was half open as was the custom when fresh, warm bread was being transported. The problem was, however, that the load was far heavier than normal and they had to push it all the way up 'The Wip', the steepest slope in Maassluis, which runs from the market square to the top of the dyke.

"I remember when we got to the market square I thought to myself, how the hell are we going to get this heavy thing up The Wip? Henk de Bruin, who was the other bloke pushing, spotted policeman Modderkolk, a German sympathiser, and he said, 'Modderkolk, Sir, you couldn't give us a hand pushing all this bread up The Wip, could you? We're just helping baker Gaasbeek out.' He agreed. If he had known what he was pushing we would have been shot on the spot."

Having arrived at the top of the dyke they thanked the policeman and the 'bread' was safely delivered to the warehouse. They breathed a massive sigh of relief that Modderkolk had never questioned the weight of the cart. When all was safe again some time later, the weapons were returned to the safety of the bank.

In our small community people tried to live as normal as possible. My father read every night to me as he had done to my sister. She was ten now and read her own books. Both my parents loved reading and instilled the importance of it into us.

At night we could hear the aeroplanes of the allies flying over on their way to Germany. My father would mention it in the morning.

"Did you hear the aeroplanes, Mien?"

"Yes, I heard them, horrible isn't it?"

"Why?" They are the allies on their way to Germany, we'll hear on the radio later what they've been up to."

"I know they're the allies and I hope they flatten another bit of Germany, but I still think it's horrible. Lots of people will be killed who don't want this war either."

Later that day it would all become clear; the RAF had bombed the industrial Ruhr or Hamburg or something else. My dad would be delighted and the pen and paper would come out and I would be despatched to somebody in the neighbourhood with the good news pinned to my vest.

Summer came again. Trips to the beaches in Hook of Holland had not been possible since the war had started because they were now no-go areas and controlled by the Germans, so nice summer days could not be spent there anymore. Not that that mattered to me because I'd never seen the beach, but it was hard on ordinary people like my parents and sister, who would have spent most warm summer Sundays there, often with other members of the family.

During the school holidays my mother would cycle there in the weekdays with my sister. Even those small pleasures were no longer possible.

I was still content. I was an avid thumb-sucker and I had a cushion with a satinette backing which I used to manipulate between my fingers. It went wherever I went even when my mother took me somewhere on her bicycle. As long as I had those pleasures I thought the world was all right.

I loved going out with my dad and cutting grass and dandelions for the rabbits, which we still kept in the backyard. I loved going to visit my aunts in the daytime with my mum, especially Aunt Alida where I could play with my cousin, who was only sixteen days younger than me.

The first time I must have noticed that things were a bit funny was at the next Saint Nicholas' Eve. My present was a wooden doll's cot, very nicely painted in bright blue and with new little sheets and a small blanket. I couldn't help but notice though, that it looked very much like the one my sister used to have and which seemed to have been missing for some time. I came to the conclusion that it was the same cot but newly painted. That was fine with me because it was now my very own. What I could not comprehend, however, was how Saint Nicholas could have got that cot out of our house, painted it and dropped it back through the chimney. Life was sometimes a complete mystery to me.

We slipped into 1943. On New Year's Day we wished the

whole family a better New Year and everybody was convinced it would now soon be over.

On my fourth birthday I became the proud owner of my sister's scooter, newly painted, of course.

6

Forced Labour

It became apparent that our Prince Bernhard occasionally managed to visit Canada where his wife Princess Juliana and two daughters were staying, because on January 19th 1943 a third daughter, Margriet Franciska, was born. This was great news for our beleaguered country and we would have put the flags out if it had been allowed. That was, of course, strictly forbidden. This glorious event brought smiles on people's faces. It was a ray of hope that some day life would be normal again.

The beginning of 1943 was very traumatic for our family. The three youngest brothers of my father had been ordered to go to Germany. Uncle Adriaan and Jo, both office workers, were told by their respective bosses, who had been ordered by the Germans to carry out this task, that they had been called up. It was a dreadful thing for these people in charge, but they had no choice. Often they also had to go themselves.

As everybody with a grain of intelligence was now an officer in the German army and was either at the front or administrating the army machine, they were terribly short of people to man the offices of their factories, which, in turn, were mostly manned by people from occupied countries, including Holland.

Uncle Arie, however, was picked up from the street on his way to work with twelve other men. They were to be sent to Germany as labourers.

The family was devastated. My mother cried. My father raged.

"The bastards just picked them up from the street, Mien, thirteen of them. What the hell is Alida going to do and the two poor kids. Mother is in a hell of a state. There wasn't even a warning. They just grabbed them. Jesus Christ, you're not even safe walking to bloody work any more. It's bad enough that Jo and Adriaan have to go leaving father, mother and Bep all on their own, but at least I'm close by. Poor Arie, he's going mad with worry. Bastard bloody Krauts."

I don't think it ever occurred to my dad that if it hadn't been uncle Arie, it would have been somebody else, but I suppose blood is thicker than water and they were a very close knit family. He had obviously also already forgotten that he himself had been very close to undergoing the same fate.

Then there was a strange twist to this tale. . . When Uncle Adriaan went to Vlaardingen to register before his departure it became clear that Uncle Arie was still registered at the address of his parents. However, he had been married for years. This was, of course, the same address as Uncle Adriaan's. The German officials got in a total muddle because they now had two people with the same initial at the same address, one an office worker and the other a labourer. That really was too much for their tiny minds. They couldn't be seen as having made a mistake, because that would have damaged their image.

Uncle Adriaan, who spoke very good German, understood every word they were saying and twigged at once what was going on. He told them that he was the labourer they were looking for and that there was only one A. van der Hoek at that address which was in fact true. The result was that he was sent to Germany to be employed as a manual worker in one of their factories and Uncle Arie was saved. Officially the other A. van der Hoek did no longer exist as far as the Germans were concerned.

That he was not a labourer was very obvious to everybody apart from the Germans; or maybe they thought it but kept it quiet. Uncle Adriaan was a slight, very smart and refined person

78

who spoke very posh Dutch while Uncle Arie was an enormous rough and tumble chap.

The family breathed a sigh of relief and in particular Aunt Alida. They were all very grateful for this act of unselfishness. It was, of course, still horrid that Uncle Adriaan and Jo had to go but at least they didn't have to leave a wife and children behind.

"Now then, off I went with the other twelve, who all kept silent about the fact that I was the wrong person," recalled my uncle at the age of 93. "Having arrived in Germany they found out pretty quickly that I was not a labourer and they didn't really know what to do with me. I told them that I was actually a correspondent who spoke German, English and French fluently, which was true. They didn't really believe that but nevertheless gave me the job as a timekeeper. The other twelve were put to work on the machines in the factory. I loved it because I was swanning around this vast place with a clipboard. I felt as if I had some sort of power over the German workers who still worked there and that made me feel really good. A sort of the reverse of what we were experiencing back home. Silly really.

"At that time they were producing vehicles for the desert war. As I indeed spoke fluent German, some of the bosses would come and sit down with me and have a cup of coffee. I used to tell them that all the mayors, now installed in Holland, were idiots and Nazis and the lackeys of the German bullies. One day one of the older people stayed behind and warned me.

" 'Adriaan, you shouldn't say things like that, it's very dangerous, everything you say is told straight to the directors. You're risking your life.'

"I told him that I only spoke the truth and that I would keep on doing so. Once I was called in by the director and warned, but it never stopped me from speaking out. Strange that, really, because I was certainly not a brave person, but the loathing I felt for them must have been stronger than my fear.

"I worried a lot about my mother and father and Bep, because with me and Jo both in Germany they were rather vulnerable. I know your dad was close by but he had his own family to care for. As it happened, Bep worked in the household of the mayor of

79

Maassluis. He was not a Nazi but obviously a German sympathiser otherwise he would not have become mayor. He must have felt sorry for Bep, because he faked a signature of a highly placed German official on a paper that stated that, as an employee of Dirkzwager, the shipping agency in Maassluis, I was vital to the German Wehrmacht (armed forces) which was, of course, nonsense because no ships could sail up the river so the services of the shipping agencies came to a complete standstill during the war. Anyway a photocopy, or blueprint, was made of the original letter and sent to me.

"I took this to the labour exchange in Brandenburg. The people in this office were all as thick as two short planks because all the intelligent people were officers in the army. When I showed them this copy they were so impressed with this newfangled proof of technology that they immediately decided that I was far too important to be kept away from my post and set me free. I had only been away three months.

"Looking back on it I had quite an interesting time, although sometimes it was very difficult and frustrating."

The whole family was overjoyed. A lot of whispering was going on in our house about the way he was released, but, of course, I was kept in the dark just in case I would blurt it out to somebody and risk the lives of the people involved. I was told that I was not to mention to anybody that uncle Adriaan was home. That was rather stupid, if you ask me, because everybody could see him, but who was I to question my parents.

Up to the time that he himself told me this tale I had always believed he had escaped. I was actually rather disappointed because I'd always thought how brave he'd been. Mind you, I was happy that he was back and to see the smiles on my grandparents faces.

Uncle Jo was not so lucky, he was away for two years and seven months and did not return until the war was well over.

He had taken a job as an office clerk at the distribution service in Maassluis, which distributed coupons and other official documents, because he had been made to believe that nobody from such offices would have to go and work in Germany. That

80

turned out to be totally false because he had only been there about three months when he was ordered to be retrained as a fitter and as soon as his schooling was finished he was to go and work in Germany.

Quite a few people from Maassluis had to go to Rotterdam to be trained. He didn't mind that because at least he was still in Holland. After they had completed the course they were told that they were to go and work in an aircraft factory in Berlin. That didn't suit Uncle Jo at all because in his opinion that was far too dangerous. The allies would certainly make it a priority to try and destroy factories like that.

He then heard a whisper that a German chap was trying to recruit people in Rotterdam to go and work in Huels in the coal-mines. With a few of his friends he went to see this man and offered him their services. They were taken on as office workers, my uncle and his mate went to Huels and the others to Essen.

The labour exchange in Maassluis was duly informed and all was well until complaints were made from Berlin because some of the 'trained fitters' had not arrived. Great confusion amongst the Germans again. The man in Rotterdam, who had taken them on, was apparently contacted and he explained that they had volunteered for the job and that they had been working in Germany for months and that it would be stupid to take them away from their present, very important occupations. That was a total lie because they had only been in Germany for a few weeks but who cared.

No more questions were ever asked and Uncle Jo stayed at the mines all the time he was in Germany.

He worked at the Augusta Vittoria mines and got the job of looking after the houses owned by the mines. He had to make sure the rents came in and that repairs where done when necessary.

Uncle Jo has always been a very happy go lucky sort of person and had never any problems getting along with people. That helped him a lot to make his time in Germany actually quite pleasant.

"We didn't work very hard mind, just pretended," he told me

81

about fifty years later. "My mate's and my living quarters were in the house of a Nazi named Rudolf. He wasn't really a bad bloke and I actually got on with him very well. I spoke adequate German, so that made life somewhat easier and sometimes, late at night, we would have a drink together and he often warned me of the danger I was in by being so outspoken, because I told them in no uncertain terms what I thought of them."

" 'One of these days Jo, they'll get you, your mouth is far too big. I'm warning you,' he would say.

"I told him that I was employed by them and that I, therefore, had the same rights as the Germans, so I could say what I liked."

" 'Not in this country you can't. You either live by the rules or you get punished. I like you, if I didn't I would have reported you ages ago.' But it never stopped me and I survived. I was treated fairly and I made, through Rudolf, quite a few friends whom I still visit."

One family, which my uncle befriended, had an eleven-year-old daughter, Inge. As uncle Jo was thirty he treated her as his little sister.

Quite a few years after the war my uncle married, but still stayed in contact with this family and sometimes visited them with his wife Annie. Unfortunately she died in 1970. He was devastated. To help him get over his grief his children suggested he visit his friends in Germany. He met Inge again and she had just divorced her husband. They fell in love and they married in 1972. On my last visit in 1999 I found them both healthy and happy, Uncle Jo now being well in his eighties. The whole family adores Inge and she is one of the very few, if not the only good thing, which came out of the war.

Both my uncles had been extremely lucky. They had been treated fairly well. Different stories were told after the war by many forced labourers. They told the terrible tales of how they had been bullied, beaten and threatened with concentration camps. They talked about long marches through snow and freezing temperatures, about journeys by train in cattle wagons, about hunger and the total lack of human care by the Germans. About lice, filth and degradation. Half a million Dutch people were sent to work for the enemy, often just picked up from the street.

Totally ignorant of any sufferings by my fellow countrymen I was a happy little girl. I was now four years old and allowed to go to nursery school. It was not very far to walk, just in the street behind my grandma's house. I loved it. There were quite a few toys to play with, paints to paint with and the teacher would often tell us stories. We played games and sang songs.

As it was a Christian school stories from the Bible were read to us. I found them fascinating. They were new to me because at home we never read from the Bible. We prayed before and after meal times, but never aloud and more out of habit than belief, I think.

My sister and I had both been christened but we hardly ever went to church. My sister had been baptised in the Dutch Reformed Church but the vicar had made such a song and dance about the fact that my father played football on Sundays that when it was my turn to be taken into the faith they chose a church which was less fussy and, whenever we happened to go to church, for instance at Christmas, we always went to the same one even after we had moved away from Maassluis to the little village of Maasland.

Life for me was great. I made friends with other little ones and I could really not see what people had to moan about. How wonderful it was to be small and innocent.

7

Bombed

Maassluis, which means sluice of the Maas, has been a place of strategic value through the ages.

Centuries ago the delta areas of the Maas and the Rhine were vast peat bogs and as far back as the 11th century the need to reclaim land for growing food became apparent.

At that time Holland, which was then only the flat, low-lying north-western part of the country, was a fiefdom of the Holy Roman Empire and was ruled by a dynasty of counts that had re-emerged after the Vikings had left.

Count Dirk II decided to drain those bogs and cultivate them. This was achieved by digging canals and ditches, which in turn took the water to the sea or the big rivers. Two of those canals discharged via two sluices into the river Maas. This created a natural harbour with a connection to the North Sea. It was called Maeslantsluys.

As we were always at loggerheads with Spain, Prince William I of Orange (William the Silent) thought Maeslantsluys so important that he had an entrenchment built there. When war with Spain broke out in 1568 (it lasted until 1648) the Spaniards arrived very quickly in this little place and overran it. They completely destroyed it in 1573, imprisoned the commander and left.

*   *   *   *

Nearly 400 years later we were in a similar position. The harbour was completely closed off from the sea, the river mined and massive concrete barricades blocked all the entrance roads to the town. The Germans were so paranoid that the allies would find a way in that they flooded large areas of farmland and erected high poles with very sharp points between the dyke and the railway to stop parachutists from landing. The only way left to harm our enemy was through the skies and that's exactly what they did.

We had been waiting for nearly three years for them to come and rescue us and we had almost given up hope. Then at half past four in the afternoon of Wednesday March 18th 1943 they came.

The roar of the RAF engines was frightening. I remember this as clear as if it happened yesterday. Hearing aeroplanes in the daytime was so unusual that everybody came out of their houses. My mother, sister and I watched together with Mrs Warnaar, our next-door neighbour. In the haste to get out of the door I had forgotten to bring my cushion, but luckily Mrs Warnaar wore a sort of satinette dress and I watched the bombs while sucking my thumb and using her dress as my cushion.

The aeroplanes flew over our houses in the direction of the harbour and then dropped their bombs, which to me looked like pieces of black cloth flying through the air. There was an awful lot of noise and very soon smoke was rising from burning buildings. The strange thing was that nobody seemed to be afraid. Everybody in our neighbourhood was outside and talking excitedly, nobody even thought of taking cover, however we certainly knew the risks.

"Let's hope they hit every boat and every damned German in the harbour," my mother said.

"Looks like it, they seem to be going in the right direction," the neighbour replied.

"God, I hope there won't be any lives lost. No Dutch lives that is, so often you hear of all the civilian casualties and so many people live at 'The Head'. I just wish I knew what was going on."

"Not a lot you can do at the moment, Mien, we'll hear soon enough. I suppose Kardien will be busy for a while with all the fires."

The reaction to this first bombardment was certainly odd. Everybody seemed so casual about it. Nobody was screaming or in a panic. It was as if we were all watching some sort of spectacle. Maybe we thought that because the people in the aeroplanes were our friends we wouldn't get hurt. Nobody went back indoors. We just hung around waiting for news. It came very quickly.

Not one German ship had been hit but several hundred metres further on our beautiful Grote Kerk (Big Church) had been severely damaged. All the houses, which stood in a circle around the church, had been destroyed. Another church was completely in ruins and the street where my father's elder brother Jan lived was flattened. When my mother heard that she nearly went mad.

"Oh my God, that's where Jan and Anna live. Dicky will be at work, but Anna must have been at home with her little boy. Oh God, what if they're dead? Jan will go insane. I wonder if he knows yet. Oh God, what is he going to do? I'd better go to mother and Bep, please look after Willy." And off she ran.

At night we heard that they were safe. Years later when both my aunt and uncle were long dead, my cousin Dicky, their daughter, recalled the story.

"My father's lunch-hour was from half past twelve until half past one and on that day, after my mother had finished the washing up and my dad had gone back to the factory, she put out the ironing board to start the weekly chore. All of sudden I remembered that a person we knew was getting married at two o'clock, so I persuaded her to go and have a look. As it was on my way to work I also decided to watch the bride and groom going up the steps of the town hall before going back to the office."

The town hall, a small, beautiful, old building, is situated on top of the dyke going from the market up the very steep slope, The Wip. Going down a gentler slope on the other side is the inner harbour, which leads to the outer harbour and the large housing estate The Head.

"Anyway, after we watched the couple entering the building she said to me that as she was now well on her way to 'The Head'

86

she might as well go and visit her mother, who lived there. My father didn't know anything about this, of course.

"Soon after the bombardment he was told that the whole street where we lived was destroyed. In a terrible panic he ran all the way to where our house had once stood and in total despair started clawing in the rubble, shouting out the names of my mum and five-year-old brother Cor. Other people were doing the same but my dad obviously didn't find anything. He had to accept the worst.

"As always when something had happened, people went to the market place. My mother, who had no idea that her house was bombed went there too, to find out for herself what was going on, leaving my brother with her mother.

"Walking past the inner harbour she could see the fires round the Big Church on the other side of the harbour and the rubble where houses had once stood. I too went to the market and found my mum. Then we spotted my dad. He was in a state of complete bewilderment. He looked dazed and as white as a sheet, believing that his wife and son were dead. Unaware of why he was like this we walked towards him and as soon as he saw us the colour seemed to flow back into his face. He ran to my mum and closed her in his arms and all he said was 'Anna, Anna' as tears started to run down his cheeks. At that moment I understood how much he loved her."

The relief at the news that both were safe was immense. I too was happy that they were alive and well because I loved this aunt and uncle very much.

"It's a miracle, Mien, it really is," said my father. "If that person hadn't got married today or if Dicky hadn't remembered, Anna and Cor would be dead by now. I just can't believe it. It can't have been their time yet."

"I know, when I heard that their street was bombed I didn't know what to do with myself. Some guardian angel was looking after them, that's for sure. I cannot begin to imagine what Jan must have felt when he saw Anna. Poor Jan, he must have nearly gone insane with worry. I wonder what will happen now, they have nothing left but the clothes they stand up in."

"They'll get help don't worry about that. They can stay with Anna's mother for a while until they find them somewhere else to live. Anyway that's not important, is it? They're alive and that's the main point. If necessary we will all have to help them a bit."

"Oh absolutely, makes you appreciate life just a little more, doesn't it?"

A few months later they were given a nice house in Maasland, a small village a few miles away from Maassluis.

Another tragic incident was the bombing of the barber's shop, which was opposite my aunt's house. All customers, including a four-year-old boy, were killed. This child's father had been sent to Germany and worked in the same factory as my Uncle Adriaan. The director summoned my uncle into his office and told him of the death of the little boy. My uncle had to go and tell this dreadful news to the father. The Germans were obviously too cowardly to do it themselves.

In total there were only eighteen people killed and four badly wounded. It could have been much worse. The bodies were laid out in the hall in one of the schools.

For us the war had changed. We now not only feared the oppressors but also the allies. We knew that they were only trying to help us, but it makes very little difference to a mother if an enemy bomb or a friendly one kills her child.

On March 22nd we were bombed again. Now we didn't watch but were lying flat on the floor under the table. My father had been horrified when my mum told him that we had actually stood outside on the first occasion and he ordered us to seek some sort of cover if it happened again.

Again no ships were hit. The rear of the PE hall of the school where the eighteen bodies were lying, awaiting the funeral, was damaged. The corpses were in the front part and were saved. In the adjoining classrooms approximately 300 children were being taught. The bombs narrowly missed them. It had been a very busy day for guardian angels.

After that we were bombed regularly, nearly always in the morning, but they often failed to do much damage to the German vessels. They hit other things round the harbour area though, in particular the water tower. Once a bomb fell in one of the reservoirs. The blast blew all the windows out of the surrounding houses and the fountain of mud coming up from the reservoir covered all those houses inside and out.

One day when we were lying again flat on the floor under the table there was an enormous bang, our house shuddered and a loud noise as if the roof had collapsed followed. I was absolutely petrified and screamed my head off.

"Stay flat on the floor," my mother warned, putting her arm around me.

When the bombardment was over, we gingerly got to our feet.

"I'm going to have a look upstairs, Willy, now you stay down here."

"But I'm frightened, I want to come with you."

"No, you wait at the bottom of the stairs, I'm going to see if everything is safe."

Slowly she climbed the stairs, looked around and saw that the roof was intact, and then she started to laugh.

"You can come up now, darling, it's OK. Some of the boxes have fallen from the loft, that's what all the noise was about."

We kept all the Christmas decorations in an enormous box and that was one of the items, which had tumbled down. On inspection we found that nearly all the glass baubles, which decorated our Christmas tree, were broken. Some sort of flying object or part of something must have hit the house. It never became clear what it was but we had certainly been very, very lucky.

Playing outside with my little friends became more difficult after that because whenever I only thought I heard an aeroplane I became hysterical.

Life was changing all the time and for the worse. Schools had to keep moving from one building to another. Materials became more and more scarce and in the end lessons were just abandoned altogether and the children stayed at home.

Food became an ever-increasing problem. Clothes were altered time after time; old coats were turned inside out and remade. Jumpers pulled out and re-knitted. Even blankets were used to make coats.

Where we were short of clothes, food and everything else you could think of, the Germans were still short of people to work in their factories. As every able German body was at the front and the Jews eradicated, their workforce had shrunk to such an extent that manufacturing became very difficult.

They now started to target the students. They were just picked up at random and 3,000 were sent to Germany. All men between eighteen and thirty-five years of age were ordered to register at labour exchanges. As very few took any notice of that, razzias were held and everybody they could lay their hands on was despatched to the Vaterland.

On March 31st the allies bombed Rotterdam again. The distant sky turned red once more with the fires. Over four hundred people perished.

The month of May saw our freedom even more restricted as nobody was allowed out after eight o'clock at night and radios were being confiscated. My father, who had no intention to lose his only link to the allies, hid his in the ceiling. It was the only way to learn of what was happening outside Holland. He knew exactly what was going on during the whole of the war, passing on this information to his friends and family.

The killings of resistance workers continued and more and more Jews were sent to camps. Over the months of May and June nearly 10,000 of them were rounded up in Amsterdam alone and sent to their deaths. Earlier in the year every Jewish orphan had been deported.

Birthdays came and went. We were still celebrating them, always visiting on the day. Now, because of the curfew, we could only visit in the daytime. The men couldn't go of course, unless it was in the weekend, but the wives and children would always turn up. It kept the family close and the spirits up.

I liked it the best when we went on the train to Vlaardingen, which was then still possible, or if the weather was fine, on the back of my mother's bicycle, my sister joining us on her own bike when her school had closed. There was always a lot of laughter and it gave a feeling of normality to the strained lives of the adults.

That summer I had the feeling that there was something odd going on in our household. It had something to do with the little shop on the corner. The owner, Mol, was in my opinion at least ninety years old. He had been to talk to my parents a few times and a very handsome, well-dressed gentleman, who lived in the posh part along our road, had also been to visit. Conversations between my parents indicated that changes were on the way.

"I've always dreamed of having a little shop, Kardien. This is such a wonderful chance."

"Yes, but what if you don't like it, we're in the middle of a bloody war, for God's sake," argued my father, who could never in all his life see the optimistic side of anything. "What about the risk we're taking, what if it's not going to work?"

"Of course it's going to work. This war is going to end one day you know and I want to achieve something, do something for me and help with the family's finances at the same time. I know I can make a success of it. I would really, really love it. You've got to take small risks sometimes. Can't you try to think positive for once in your life?"

"I have to get a trader's certificate; that's not going to be easy, is it?"

"Oh, for God's sake, all you ever see are problems. Dirk Pons (he was the posh gentleman) told you, he'll instruct you. Anyway, as long as there is a war on you don't have to worry about that."

Conversations like this were now the order of the day and they sometimes ended in a full-blown row.

Despite all the horrors of the war, the lack of food and almost anything else you could think of, my mother's spirits were high and all she could see was a bright future in a little corner shop.

We moved at the end of the summer in 1943.

8

The Shop

Moving house was a horrible experience for me. I really could not understand why we couldn't stay where we were. Everything had to be packed up, the house was a total mess and I seemed to be forever in everybody's way. The only time I was spoken to was when I did something wrong or was yet again in the wrong place.

"Willy, go and stand somewhere else. Willy, leave that alone. Willy don't touch that. Willy, if you want to be useful go and take that to the new house." That's all I heard from my father, mother and sister. What they didn't seem to understand was that I wanted everything to stay as it was. My stupid sister seemed to be actively involved in the move and was probably enjoying herself but I felt totally and utterly abandoned and depressed. Thank God for my thumb and my cushion! I suppose I was lucky that they hadn't packed that up as well.

As there were only three houses in between the shop and the house we were abandoning there was no need for a removal firm to give us a hand. Everything was just hand carried. A few of my father's friends helped carrying the heavy things and my mum and sister carried boxes and the lighter stuff. I carried my doll's cot and some of my other toys and put them in the front bedroom which I was to share with my sister. I decided very quickly that I did not like the house at all. As a matter of fact I hated it.

The shop door, which was also our front door, was right on the

92

corner of our and my grandmother's street. To get to the living quarters you had to walk through the shop.

The shop itself was quite small. It had two windows, one in our street and one in grandma's which my mother used to decorate beautifully. Behind the counter were the racks that carried the stock, which was already rather diminished by then, and big wooden trays for sugar, salt and all other things that were sold loose.

The living-room was bigger than in our old house, but there was no front room, so all the furniture had to be crammed into this one space. We had quite a big alcove to the side of the room where a cupboard-bed had once been. The very steep stairs were in the tiny corridor between the shop and the living-room.

The upstairs was exactly the same as in our old house. One bedroom, the large open space on top of the stairs and a loft space all around that. The kitchen was a little larger. Built onto this was a ramshackle conservatory, which went straight into the very large area of the 'waterstokerij', the part of the business where we sold hot water. It had an enormous boiler, which was fired by wood and coke. Hot water was sold by the bucket.

At the far end of this area was another small corridor where our toilet was; the seat being a rectangular wooden plank with a hole in the middle. On a nail in the wall hung the toilet paper which were square pieces of newspaper strung on a piece of string. It was quite awful. It was cold, dark and damp. We had no outside at all and that was therefore the end of keeping rabbits. A large door in this boiler-room came out into my grandmother's street.

This boiler-room was also used as a shed, and the bicycles, the sink tubs and all sorts of other stuff was neatly kept in there. A few shelves near the massive tap contained soap powders, washing soda, little sachets of blue powder that people used in the rinsing water to make the whites look whiter, and other items needed to do the weekly laundry. Most people bought those items at the same time as the hot water.

One very good thing was that on Friday nights, when we all had a bath in the boiler room, you could use as much hot water as you liked. We placed the sink tub under the tap and when the

93

water got a bit cold, you could just put some more hot into it. I absolutely loved that bit. It was also great for my mum to do the washing, as there was always hot water galore.

When we took over the shop my mum and dad decided that they would only sell hot water on Mondays for the washing, and on Fridays for bathing. The previous owner had sold it every day and even delivered it in small barrels. He loaded them on a little cart which he pulled behind his bicycle, but that was too much for us as my mum was the only person to run the show.

On these two days my dad had to get up very early in the morning to light the boiler before he went to work. Women would come with their buckets, sometimes three or four times, depending on how much hot water they needed or how big their washing load was. Everything was washed by hand, of course, because washing machines were still unheard of in our society. On Fridays it depended on how many people there were in their family. Sometimes children were washed one after the other in the same bath water but that didn't happen in our house. We always had a tub with clean water all to ourselves even before we moved to the shop.

It took a few days before the house was organised and then my mum started on the shop. She was in her element. She cleaned and polished and arranged her meagre wares neatly. She dressed the two shop windows, put on her best white, starched apron and then was ready for business.

One thing about all this stands out in my mind. For the first time in my young life I had to go to sleep in an unmade bed. There hadn't been enough time for that I'm afraid! I thought that was terrible and I certainly felt very neglected.

Luckily I'm never unhappy for very long and, of course, I got quickly used to the change and I loved it when my mum allowed me to help her in the shop. It was all quite a challenge for her, even more so because of the coupons.

At that time salesmen were still calling to take orders and I loved it when the goods came in and I could help unpack.

My mother had one strict rule: she would not sell to the Germans. They hardly ever came in the shop in any case, but one who was billeted in a house near us would sometimes come in. He was actually a very sweet man who had a family in Germany and didn't want to be in the war, but even so my mother refused to sell to him. Luckily he understood. One could be shot for lesser offences.

The woman with whom this German was billeted also felt sorry for him, but her husband forbade her to even speak to him. If you had enough room in your house you were ordered to take in one or more soldiers, if you liked it or not. If you refused they simply kicked you out altogether.

One day, to show them that he only meant to do his best for them, he brought home three real cream cakes. But the husband would not eat this treat and told his wife not to either.

"I felt so sorry for this poor man. He only did his best and tried to be friendly and to be honest I could have murdered a cream cake, but no, I wasn't allowed to eat it," she told my mum in the shop.

"He tries to have a conversation with my husband, but he just totally ignores him, as if he doesn't exist and when I show signs of trying to answer him I get such a look that I daren't open my mouth. I must admit I think it's all a bit exaggerated. Gosh, after all, he is a human being, isn't he?"

"Yes, I can see how difficult it must be for you, he is quite a nice chap actually, but I can also understand your husband. He is, nice or not nice, still a German. He's been in the shop, you know, but I won't sell anything to him. I feel a bit sorry for him too, but I've made a stand and I won't change my mind, whatever he's like he is our enemy. I should just talk to him when your husband isn't there and try to explain to him what a nightmare it is for you. Anyway, what happened to the cream cakes?"

"He took them to his room, must have eaten all three of them. God my mouth starts to water just thinking about biting into some real cream."

"Stop it, you're making mine water too." They both laughed and when the lady left the shop she shouted:

"I'll ask him to bring you some."

When my mother related the story to my dad, he thought it was hilarious. No need to say that the whole family was informed.

My mother soon found out that quite a few people came in the shop just for a chat. They would buy something, of course, but then stopped talking for about half an hour. That didn't suit my mum at all. So if certain people came in and stopped too long I had to shout something out like, 'mum the milk is boiling', or she would make another excuse to get away from them. She had, after all, also a house to run. My dad still came home every lunch-time and she had to get some sort of a meal ready. The shop closed from twelve-thirty until two o'clock so we could have our meal in peace and my mum could relate what had happened in the morning.

Even in the shop I got myself into trouble sometimes. My mother gave many of the people in the neighbourhood nicknames. In the house next door to the shop lived an old woman. She was a cantankerous old biddy who was always dressed in a brown raincoat and a brown hat. My mother had therefore christened her 'Little Hat'. Nobody in our household called her anything else and to this day I have no idea what her real name was.

Sometimes when my mother was busy doing something in the house I would mind the shop and call her when a customer came in. So when this woman came in one day I said hello and then shouted at the top of my voice, "Mum, Little Hat is here." The looks I was given by my mother and Little Hat could have killed me but I had no idea what I'd done wrong. I was severely reprimanded and told that you didn't mention people's nicknames. Well, how was I supposed to know it wasn't her real name? After that I would just say that there was a customer, nothing much could be wrong with that.

The war was still raging. We were still being bombed and when that happened we had to lie flat on our stomachs in the alcove. I never got used to the bombings and never failed to scream my head off all through the raids.

My father's radio sat now in a different ceiling and he listened to it whenever it was deemed safe, but for a while my mum didn't seem interested in the war, the shop was more important than

96

anything else to her. It was a wonderful, however temporary, diversion for all of us.

I was still only four and occasionally I woke up in the night and wanted a wee. That had never been a problem in our old house because the toilet was in the kitchen. My mum or dad would go down with me with a torch. We couldn't switch the light on upstairs just in case a little beam would escape through the blackout curtains. But we could in the kitchen because nobody could see that. I even could do that on my own.

This house was very different though, no way was I going on my own through the boiler-room to that horrid toilet. My dad got out of bed and carried me, torch in hand. When we came to the boiler-room I was struck dumb with horror. The whole floor was a moving carpet of cockroaches. Even my dad was appalled. I screamed my head off and wet myself at the same time. My mother came stumbling down in the dark.

"What's going on, what's the matter with Willy?"

"The whole floor in the boiler-room is covered with cockroaches, it's awful," explained my dad. "Go and see for yourself, here take the torch, I can't take her to the loo through that, anyway it's too late."

"Oh, Jesus. What are we going to do about this? I won't go through that either. Where have they all come from?"

"It's always warm in there, isn't it? They hide in the day and come out at night. We'll have to do something. I'll ask around tomorrow. Better tell Dicky as well just in case she needs a wee in the night."

"I'll dig out the potty, we'll have to use that in future until we get rid of those horrid things."

My mother found me a clean nighty and still in a state of shock I was put back to bed.

The potty was found and positioned in a corner in the space where my parents slept.

As I explained earlier, the houses in our street were only separated from the dyke by a small road. On top of the dyke is the

97

main road that runs from Hook of Holland all the way to Rotterdam. Now this road is only used by locals and cyclists coming through Maassluis on their way to the beach in Hook of Holland as motorways have replaced all these small, provincial ones.

At night the Germans patrolled this road during blackout. By doing so they could overlook an enormous part of the estate and if light was seen punishment could be severe.

We had a single light bulb hanging just on top of the stairs which served as a light for my parents sleeping space and my sister's and my bedroom. Light bulbs were no longer available, so you used as few as you could.

One night I needed a wee. I called out and my mum came and fetched me, in the dark, of course. Just to see where the potty was she switched the light on, put me on it and switched it off again. A minute later there was a loud hammering on the shop door, not just knocking, but more like somebody trying to break the door down. It was accompanied by loud shouting to open the door. We were all frozen with fear. It even woke my sister.

"What's happening Mum?"

"Please go straight back to bed and stay where you are." Without a word she disappeared back into the room and crawled into her bed shaking with fear.

My father went down, in his vest and long underpants; the men in our circles did not wear pyjamas in those days and dressing gowns were totally unheard of. I was still sitting on the potty in the dark, too frightened even to cry. We heard my father unlocking the door.

"*Sie haben das Licht eingeschalten, dass ist strengstens verboten, wo ist es?*"(You've switched the light on, that's strictly forbidden, where is it?) My father, who didn't understand a word of German, knew, however, exactly what he meant and pointed upstairs.

With a massive torch this vile, fat, leather booted German ran upstairs, his heavy footwear making the most awful din on every tread. My mother tried to explain and pointed at me. He shouted out something to my mother treating her as if she had committed a murder. He then unscrewed the bulb, returned downstairs and out into the street where he smashed it right outside the shop door. For the rest of the war and beyond we had no light upstairs. I have never forgotten nor forgiven the Germans for this pathetic, childish, power crazed gesture. It left us all shaking with fear and my mother shaking with rage and there was nothing we could do about it.

We were fortunate, however, to be still together as a family. Thousands and thousands of men were now in Germany or in hiding from the Germans, either to avoid being sent to work for them or because they were sought for their part in illegal acts against the regime.

Thousands of Jews were being hidden and, of course, allied pilots and crews from planes that had been shot down.

There was a countrywide organisation, which coordinated a network of hiding places all over the country. The leader was a vicar, the reverend Frits Slomp, who called himself Frits the Wanderer.

Their biggest problem was not so much finding hiding places but how to obtain food and money for those people. To be able to obtain coupons you had to show your identity card. Those people couldn't do that because if they showed their cards they would be caught and often executed; if they were Jews deportation to the gas chambers was unavoidable.

False papers were needed and they were produced by the thousand. The most urgent problem, however, was to get hold of coupons quickly. The only way out was stealing them from the distribution centres.

Two men, a student and his brother who worked at the centre, executed the first raid on such a place. It took place in a small village in Friesland in the Northeast of the country and thousands of these valuable little stamps were handed to the organisation to be used for the people in hiding. Many more such raids followed, even in our town.

On April 10th 1944 the whole town was in uproar. My father was overjoyed.

"Mien, they've raided the distribution office, have you heard? Another one in the eye for those bastards. Nobody knows who did

99

it, but they think that Huisman, the police sergeant, was involved. They're looking for them everywhere but I bet they've long disappeared to somewhere safe. I bet they'll be issued with false papers pretty soon."

"Yes I've heard. I just hope they will never get caught because if they do they'll lose their lives and that's for sure. There are certainly some brave people about. The only thing is will we still get our coupons though? I've heard they've taken at least two months' supply."

"Don't worry about that they just get other ones."

"Oh good, because if I'm not getting any coupons I can't get any food nor stock either."

He was right. On April 13th the office was back in working order and everybody got their coupons.

Stories like these warmed the heart of every true Dutchman. Only the day before an English aeroplane had crashed near our town. Two of the crew survived and fled. All roads were blocked and police searched everywhere. They were never found. Spirited away by the locals to one of the farms in the surrounding country-side; but it meant two more mouths to feed without coupons.

The planning for the raid on our distribution centre had started months before it was executed. One of the police sergeants in Maassluis, Jacob Huisman, had already been approached by Frits Slomp in August 1943 and asked to do something for the hundreds of people who were hiding in and around our town.

The local part of this Country Organisation (help for people in hiding) organised false papers, food and often work for these men and women. As soon as they had been issued with their false identities they were put to work and many were working on the conversion of an old warehouse in Maassluis, which was to become the new reformed church, replacing the one that had been totally destroyed by the bombing on May 10th 1943. Work was found for them on farms and other sympathising industries.

This organisation had their ears to the ground at all times and any important information or warnings would filter very quickly through to most parts of the country.

The news came that a big razzia was in the offing to find

100

people who were hiding on the farms in Maasland, a small village near our town. When the razzia took place all they found on one farm were some small bags of Belgium shag and a radio, which by now was illegal. The farmer and his wife were arrested. The Germans did not find any of the people who were hiding in that area.

Jacob Huisman was approached again, this time to help with the raid on the distribution office. It had been rumoured that the safe where the coupons were kept was impossible to crack as the walls were reinforced concrete, the steel door equipped with a time clock and a very loud alarm system. A policeman from Maasland, however, who had accompanied distribution clerks on several occasions, had said that the ceiling was only plaster. It would be dead easy to enter from the roof of the safe.

Jacob Huisman racked his brain but could not find a way to let the men into the building without bloodshed until fate gave a helping hand. On April 6th he discovered that his duties and roster were to be changed. He would be guarding the safe from six o'clock in the morning until two o'clock in the afternoon, starting on Easter Sunday. He was to share his shift with one other sergeant. A frantic time of contacting everybody and making plans arrived.

The raid was planned for Easter Monday morning. His first shift on Easter Sunday was spent agonising over the coming dangerous event. As soon as he got home after finishing his shift he was called back on duty to search for the two Englishmen from the shot down plane. Needless to say he didn't find them. Even if he had he would have made sure they found a safe home.

A last secret meeting was held in the middle of the night and the plans discussed in detail.

Next morning, after a sleepless night, he arrived at his post. His colleague, who knew nothing of this raid, was already there. When Huisman slid the bolts noisily across the door to secure it, he slid them back again, leaving the door open before he joined his colleague in the safe room.

"Morning, Grootendorst."

"Morning, Huisman, cold and dark this morning isn't it? I find this duty pretty boring, don't you?"

"Yes, rather," said Huisman, thinking it won't be boring for

101

long. He offered Grootendorst his tobacco pouch and said, "Roll yourself a fag, I've got to go to the loo."

He went down and opened the door. One of the gang appeared.

"Listen, I'm going to pull the flush and then you can all follow me up the stairs in your socks. Each man had a pistol which had been smuggled by the wife of one of the gang from The Hague hidden under her clothing.

On hearing the flush they crept up the stairs and when they reached the top of the stairs, according to plan, they grabbed Huisman and bound him and then Grootendorst who, by then, was in a total state of shock.

The ceiling was quickly demolished and the coupons loaded in sacks and bound onto their bicycles. Huisman pretended to protest loudly when they told him to go with them, but his bicycle including a bag with civilian clothes was waiting for him. They fled in haste with their loot of around 20,000 coupon cards.

Huisman's fiancée and his parents were arrested along with twenty distribution clerks. The clerks were quickly released, the fiancée was set free a month later but Huisman's parents were locked up separately in a concentration camp from which they were eventually released, unharmed, in September 1944.

Huisman had now himself become one of the many people in hiding. He obtained a new identity card and became known as Arend Vermeulen. For a long time he lived with the family whose two sons had found the two Englishmen whose aeroplane had crashed in Maassluis. They had found them hiding in a chicken run. They took one each on the back of their bikes and transported them to a safe haven. They hid them until they were spirited back to England.

We had celebrated another Saint Nicholas, another Christmas and I had seen my fifth birthday. Rations were getting smaller and smaller. Everything went to Hitler's 'Totalkrieg' (total war). The items for sale in our shop dwindled. Less and less salesmen were calling but the worst was still to come.

9

Hot Milk

My mother was a very good amateur actress. She had been an active member of the local amateur dramatic society for years but all this stopped in February 1942. The Germans had ordered all actors, professional and amateur, to register at the Chamber of Culture which meant that they could only perform plays which had been approved by this chamber.

The members of my mother's group, without any exceptions, decided that they did not want to be part of anything slightly German and that they certainly did not want to be told by anybody what sort of plays they could or could not put on. They decided to disband and wait for better times to come. It would have also been difficult to find a venue as the cinema-cum-theatre was now only for the Germans.

As she loved acting and singing she decided that she would entertain the neighbourhood in these dark times. Life had become very dull for the adults because they couldn't go to the cinema unless they went with a German, radios had been confiscated, although my dad's and many others were still hidden in ceilings or other safe places, and all form of other entertainment had long stopped. So my mum decided to do it herself.

As we had now very little to sell in the shop she had time on her hands. It would also keep my sister amused, who was at home as all schools had been closed. We were to have a performance in our boiler-room.

My cousin, the other Willy van der Hoek, who was only a couple of weeks younger than me, was also in on the act. My mother and sister chose a few well-known songs which they would sing together, and my cousin and I were to perform to them. There was one about dwarfs and the things they get up to in the middle of the night when the little children are asleep, and we had to act out all their good deeds. We had spades, rakes, brooms, buckets and whatever was needed to perform the chores.

The one I remember best though, was about a little boy who found a single rose on the moor. He is mesmerised by its beauty and wants to keep it forever so he picks it and the little rose dies. It was a rather sad song and I remember I cried for the little rose when I first heard it. I must have done quite a lot of crying in my young days.

My sister and my mum sang it beautifully. I was the little boy and had to dance gracefully round the rose, which was my cousin, and admire it and act out all the other words of the song. My cousin only had to sway gently but in the end had to die with as much grace as could be expected from a five-year-old.

After quite a few rehearsals we were ready for the afternoon performance. Costumes had been fashioned from old curtains, dresses and crêpe paper and were neatly laid out in the living-room, which doubled as a dressing-room. My mother invited all the women in the street, including my grandmother and Aunt Bep and Aunt Alida, my cousin's mother, was, of course, also present and on the day they came carrying their own chairs. There must have been about fifteen of them.

My mother and sister had decorated the boiler-room somewhat and built a stage from upturned boxes and anything else they could find.

It was a roaring success and we had to do everything twice and every time the audience clapped loudly and cheered. Instead of going home straight away after the performance they all stayed on for a while enjoying the happy atmosphere.

"That was the best afternoon I've had for ages Mrs Hoek (they often left off the 'van der'), thanks very much."

"Thanks for all the trouble; haven't enjoyed myself so much for a long time."

"Aren't those two little girls good actresses and you and Dicky sang so well."

"I hope you will do that again. What a great time I've had."

Many comments like these were made and we were grateful for being able to forget the hardships of our daily lives for a couple of hours.

Food was now very scarce and people tried to obtain things from the farmers in the surrounding countryside by swapping their jewellery, bed-linen or any other precious commodity for milk, potatoes or whatever was available. Massive queues formed every day to cross the river to Rozenburg and farmers were inundated with people asking for help.

Sometimes when the farmers had harvested their crops of wheat they would let people on the land to 'read' the field, which meant that they could gather the ears that had been left behind. My mum and dad did that as well. At home they would thrash the ears and then take it to the open fields behind the estate and let the wind take the husk. A tiny bit of wheat was the result, which was then ground up somehow, probably in the coffee grinder. It would then be mixed with water and made into some kind of porridge. Milk was no longer available.

I had always been a small child but by now I was very thin. My Aunt Nel, my father's sister, who had a weak spot for me, was quite alarmed when she saw me.

"Look, Mien, why don't you send her to me every morning for a beaker of milk. We still have the cow and we can spare some for Willy. She is so thin, it really worries me," she said to my mum.

"That would be wonderful, Nel, I'm worried about her too. However, she's lively enough."

"Yes, I can see that, but anyway send her around eleven and the maid (they were the only ones in the family who had a maid) can see to her."

I was dreading it. I had never liked milk very much so to me the lack of it was no hardship. I had no choice in the matter, of course. Off I went the next morning. It wasn't very far and I could easily do this on my own.

I liked my aunt very much and was looking forward to seeing her or one of her three daughters who were older than me, or even Hannie her little toddler with whom I liked playing.

When I got there only the maid seemed to be in. She was a sour, unfriendly sort of person and I'm sure she felt that I came to steal the food out of her mouth. When I told her I had come for a beaker of milk, she barked:

"I know, I have been told."

She frightened the living daylights out of me and made me feel even smaller than I already was. I was only five years old and I didn't even want the blooming stuff. She begrudgingly reheated the milk, poured it in the beaker and handed it to me.

The first thing I noticed was a big skin floating in it, and if there was one thing I hated more than anything it was a skin in or on the milk. When we could still buy milk my mother always used a little strainer when she poured milk for me. I tried to drink it but every time this vile object got in the way and made me heave. I don't think that there was anything worse in the whole world at that moment than this terrible slippery skin. I tried to fish it out with my fingers but the dirty look I got from this awful maid made me give it up. By now I was close to being sick and tears were pricking in my eyes. I hated this hot milk. I even hated the smell of it and no way could I swallow this slippery obstacle. In the end I stuck one finger in the beaker and somehow held back the skin and drank the rest.

As soon as I had finished it I left and ran all the way home swearing I would never go again. But I had no choice. After a few more days I took courage and spoke to the maid.

"Please could you strain the milk for me, I hate the skins, they make me feel really sick."

"Don't be so ungrateful, you little madam. The skins are the best of the milk. You should be pleased your aunt is giving you any milk at all; she doesn't have to do this you know. I will certainly not strain it for you. Either drink the lot or leave it, you

106

horrid little child."

Tears pricked behind my eyes again, but I would not let this silly maid see it. I took my beaker into the living-room to get away from the prying eyes of this awful woman. There was nobody else in the room.

A large skin was yet again floating in my beaker. Desperate to get rid of it I fished it out and placed it neatly behind one of the easy chairs. Nobody would notice, I thought. Unfortunately my aunt walked in and sat down in the chair opposite. She was rather a formidable lady; tall and sturdy, with enormous breasts. I loved her very much but I was, at the same time, quite in awe of her and would never have dreamed of being cheeky or rude to her.

"Whatever is that behind that chair?" she asked.

"Where Aunty? I can't see anything."

"Well, I can." And with that she got up and found the skin. I was very frightened and tears started to run down my face. I don't think I'd ever felt so miserable.

"Did you put it there, Willy?" she asked sternly.

"Well you see, I don't mind drinking the milk but the skins are so terrible I can't swallow them. They make me feel sick and the maid won't take them out for me," I sobbed.

"Well, you are a very naughty girl and I shall tell your dad. Don't ever do that again or you won't be getting any milk at all."

I would have loved to say that I hated her bloody milk and that she could keep it as far as I was concerned but, of course, I didn't dare. My father was duly informed and he gave me a telling off, while my mum thought it was hilarious.

"Well it's not her fault is it? Why can't this stupid maid use a strainer? I'm sure she does it out of spite. God, you would think it was her blooming cow," said my mother.

"You might well be right Mien, but that child should be a bit more grateful, Nel is only doing her best after all," answered my dad.

I have a feeling that because my aunt and uncle were much better off than the rest of the family, they had to be treated with respect in my father's eyes, while my mother, who had been in service for many years, thought differently about the well off.

107

It was already known that my uncle, who was a fruit and vegetable wholesaler, was supplying the Germans. It was hushed up in the family because he did make sure my grandparents had enough to eat.

About ten days after this incident we were told that the cow was to be slaughtered. Never have I been so pleased about the death of an animal. I have never drunk milk since; the smell of boiled milk still makes me heave.

We still had a cat in those days. It was fed on scraps and must have supplemented its rations by catching mice in the fields. My father wasn't always home at mealtimes because of the strange hours they had to work when they were on fire watch. He would have his warm meal when he came in.

One day my mother had managed to get some minced meat from which she had made four minuscule meatballs. The one for my dad was a little larger than ours. She had dished out his meagre rations on a plate at the start of our meal, to be warmed up later. When we finished she had put it in the kitchen while she cleared the rest of the table.

Then there was an awful commotion. My sister and I ran to the kitchen where my mother was nearly strangling the cat.

"You bloody stupid animal, look what you've done, that's all there was to eat for the poor man. Get out before I kill you," my mother screamed, kicking the cat at the same time. The cat flew away screaming with the last crumbs of the meatball still hanging in his whiskers.

My sister and I were stunned. We knew what it meant to my mother. No meat for our dad. My mum sat down and cried. Her small head buried in her hands. Her short, dark hair bobbing up and down with the rhythm of her sobs. It was, for once, all too much for her.

It is now difficult to imagine what a tragedy it was. For the first time in my young life I realised how hard she tried to feed us all properly, often going without herself. It made me very sad and all I could do was hug her while tears started rolling down my cheeks. In later years we laughed about this incident, but at the time it was a major disaster. There is no need to say that my father, who didn't like the cat much anyway, was not a happy man. The cat was given some unusual names and Dad had to be satisfied with a bit of bread instead of his meatball.

People who had money could still buy things on the black market but we had no money and certainly could not afford DFL64.00 for a kilo of lard, which was then approximately £6.50 in wartime England. We had nothing to swap either.

Occasionally my father worked overtime and my sister would go to the factory to take him his food. A couple of times he took her to a secret place where he had hidden one of the small doormats which were being made in his place of work.

"Look Dicky, I've a little mat here, maybe Mum can swap it for a bit of milk."

"How am I going to take that home, I can't just carry it under my arm. Everybody will see it."

"No, I know, I'll tie it round your middle and your coat will hide it."

"That's never going to work."

"Of course it will. Come here, I've got some string."

He tied the mat round my sister's waist and covered it all up with her buttoned up coat.

She had to walk home very upright as the stiffness of the mat prohibited her from bending. That it made her look like an arthritic Michelin man would never have occurred to my dad. My mother fell about laughing when she saw her the first time.

"Whatever is the matter with you? You're walking like a statue. What have you got under your coat?"

"Shush Mum, it's a doormat. Dad thinks we can swap it maybe for some milk. Can you take it off me because the bristles are hurting me something terrible."

"Oh, you poor child, trust your dad to lumber you with it. God, your father actually nicked it did he? Bless him, we might get something for it if we're lucky."

109

My father was a very honest man, but he was desperate and he saw this act of thieving only as a means of helping his family.

Then a time of joy overtook the gloom and doom of those awful days. My father was jubilant and listened to every word on radio Oranje, repeating it all to my mother in whispers. It was June 6th 1944.

"Mien, the allies have landed in Normandy, at last they've come. I bet they'll be swarming all over the place soon. It will probably be all over long before the winter. That will wipe the smiles off those Krauts' faces. Maybe it will stop the bastards singing and marching through my town."

"God, wouldn't that be wonderful. Are they in France did you say? How long do you think it will take them to get here? It must be an enormous task for them to fight their way into Holland all the way from France.

"Yes, I know that Mien, but they might be landing in other places soon, there's no stopping them now, I tell you. God, this is such good news I can hardly believe it. Just think, we will soon be free. Better send Willy on her round."

I carried many messages in those days as I was still the safest courier. People were all of a sudden more optimistic about the future. There was laughter and it seemed as if people had straightened their backs. They couldn't show their joy outside though, as they were not supposed to know what was happening.

To me, however, as a five-year-old, the names of the towns in France which were being freed meant nothing. For me it was just another summer. I played outside with my little friends. We built tents with blankets draped over clothes-horses. Sometimes they were our houses, sometimes it was a hospital and the dolls were the patients. We played with the few toys we had. We went for walks and picked flowers, we played hide and seek, we played with marbles or skipping ropes.

We still visited our relatives and did the shopping, however meagre the rations were. I still loved going to my grandparents. To me life hadn't changed much. My town was still swarming with singing, marching, obnoxious Germans, but even that was normal to me because I had never known it to be any different. I

110

wasn't even hungry. I was just getting thinner.

The euphoria stayed and when the allies entered Belgium the Dutch could hardly keep the smiles from their faces. My little legs were worn out with carrying messages. Every time new towns had been freed their names were written on the pieces of paper. On September 6th my father nearly exploded with happiness.

"Mien, Mien, listen they've freed Breda. They're in Holland. They poured over the map again, following the towns falling to the hands of the allies.

"Look, see, that's Antwerp and now Breda, not far to Rotterdam now. They think it might all be over by Christmas."

My sister was also allowed to look at the map, she had obviously heard of all those names. When I tried to get a look in I was just pushed out of the way. In moments like that I felt rather left out and I accused my sister of being a bloody know-all, not out loud, of course. All I was good for was carting messages around. The world was rather unfair to me, I thought.

The rumour of the liberation of Breda and the speed with which the allies were advancing started circulating on September 5th and was announced by the BBC on the same evening. That this rumour was actually false nobody knew until the next day.

The announcement of the advance sent shock waves through the ranks of the NSB people and other German collaborators. Mussert, who was the leader of the NSB organisation removed his wife, his second cousin, who was also his mistress, her mother and some friends from Amsterdam and took them to Holten, a tiny place in the province of Drente and not far from Westerbork, the dreaded place where thousands of Jews had been sent for onward transportation to the gas chambers.

The news that Mussert had fled put the fear of God into the NSB community in Amsterdam. In total panic they fled en masse to Westerbork, which was now empty, and from there poured into Germany. This day was later called 'Dolle Dinsdag' (Frantic Tuesday). It was an exodus of more than 65,000 people. It wasn't long before all the houses and shops belonging to these traitors were plundered.

111

Expectations of being liberated soon remained high. When news of the big push started circulating on September 17th spirits soared and the trains stopped running.

10

A Bridge Too Far

The euphoria continued when Maastricht in Limburg, the most southerly province of The Netherlands, was freed. The allies were still pushing on, or so we thought. The truth was, however, slightly different. By now the supply lines to the troops had become too long. Every gallon of petrol, every piece of ammunition, every mouthful of food had to be transported from the French ports. The journey was too long and too slow. To be able to continue their push they had to open the supply route through the Wester Schelde, south of the island of Walcheren in the province of Zeeland. This was, however, postponed to give priority to operation Market Garden.

When this battle for the three bridges over the Maas, Waal and Neder-Rijn started on September 17th our hopes were higher than ever before that freedom was in sight

News of victories in Grave, Eindhoven and Nijmegen brought feelings of utter relief for the Dutch population but sent shock waves through the German command. Out of revenge they bombed Eindhoven just after it had been freed and 225 people lost their lives.

The allies had taken Antwerp and this vital harbour was now in their hands. This was an enormous setback for the enemy. They became so paranoid that out of sheer frustration they bombed and completely destroyed the harbour of Amsterdam just in case;

even before the battle near Arnhem was finished. On September 23rd Rotterdam harbour was blown to pieces. No transport via the harbours was now possible.

When the allied troops landed near Arnhem the Dutch Government in London ordered, via the BBC, a total strike of all railway personnel. This was done to prevent troops and supplies being transported to the front. A plan for the complete closing down of the railways had been in place for quite some time, but when at last the order came without any prior warning, it surprised staff of all ranks.

It was an extremely dangerous thing to do for the workers because striking meant the death penalty when you were caught. After a few days of total and utter confusion the whole railway network had come to a complete standstill and 30,000 railway personnel went in hiding. They thought it would only be for a few weeks. It lasted for nearly eight months.

The Germans, in a desperate attempt to keep the trains going for their own use, brought 4,500 men from Germany to operate them because they were vital for the transport of food to the front. They were now so short of transport that out of desperation they started to requisition privately owned cars, barges and even bicycles.

Then disaster struck. No explanation is necessary, as everybody knows the story about the 'bridge too far' at Arnhem. Nobody ever believed that the allies could fail. But fail they did. When the news broke on September 27th the population was devastated. They grieved for the loss of so many brave soldiers who had tried so hard to reach us. They grieved because they knew it would now be a long time before they would regain their freedom, if it would ever happen at all. They despaired. They were also frightened because they knew that reprisals would follow.

Our family was in a state of shock. My father's elation changed to desperation.

"Oh bloody hell, Mien, now what will happen to us. I was so

114

sure it was all over."

"They'll be back, they'll try something else, they've come so far, they won't give up now," said my mother.

"Mien, they will take it out on us. Half the country is free, everything south of the Rijn is free and we're cut off from where the action is. Don't you understand those bastards want revenge?"

And revenge they wanted indeed. Even for the smallest misdemeanours. The story about Putten, a small town north-west of Arnhem, in the same province of Gelderland, emerged.

More and more acts of sabotage were carried out by small groups of resistance workers. In Putten they assaulted a German lorry in the middle of the night. The lorry contained four members of the Luftwaffe (German air force). They took one of them. Out of revenge for this act the Germans vented their anger on this small town. Every man between eighteen and fifty they could find was taken and they were hoarded together at the end of the day in the Dutch Reformed Church, 650 were sent to a camp in Amersfoort. What they did to those innocent people does not bear thinking about but the fact that only forty-nine survived speaks for itself. As if that wasn't enough more than a hundred houses and buildings were set alight. After that Putten was called the Town of Widows. German cruelty knew no bounds.

For us, in the west of the country, the collapse of operation Market Garden was catastrophic. The railway strike had so infuriated Seyss-Inquart, the Reichskommissar (state commissioner), who ruled our country, that he tried to break it by starving the population.

We were now cut off from the south of the country where the coal-mines were, because that part was already free. So we had no fuel. Even if the Germans would have allowed us access, which they didn't, there was no longer any transport. Wheat and potatoes had to come from the north and east of the country which was still occupied and the Germans forbade any transport of food to the west.

Our rations were very soon at starvation level, less than 500 calories a day. Soup kitchens had been introduced. The soup consisted of yellowish water with a few cabbage leaves floating in it and if you were lucky a few bits of potato.

Long queues formed at The Head to get across to the islands where a little flour, some potatoes or maybe some bread might be obtained. People walked from Rotterdam or rode on bicycles without tyres. They arrived with little carts and waited sometimes for days to get across because the big ferry was now only for the Germans and the people had to get across in a large rowing boat.

My sister often went with one of her friends in search of food. My mother worried about her a lot and when she was about to set off on one of her quests the same dialogue would take place.

"Please be careful darling, don't take risks and you know what to do when they start bombing."

"Yes Mum, I have to lie flat on the ground, I've done it before, don't worry."

My mother's face had started to show the signs of stress. Her eyes had lost their sparkle, her thin nose was looking more pointed, her now very thin face pale and drawn. Tears would well up into her eyes when she had to hand me a piece of sugarbeet instead of a proper slice of bread. As it happened I quite liked sugarbeet, to me it was a normal part of my diet but sometimes we didn't even have that.

On the way to Hook of Holland, below the dyke were and still are, large farms, producing wheat and vegetables. Quite near to Hook of Holland is Oranje Sluys, which was a German post during the war. Nobody was allowed through. Children had found out, however, that by cycling very fast and shouting out 'Rosenkohl' (sprouts) the Germans would let them pass. They knew that they were just trying to get some food and they never harmed them.

"Mum, I've heard there are some sprouts by Oranje Sluys. I'm going with Map Spek," my twelve-year-old sister announced one day.

"OK darling, but be careful and stay together."

Off they went on their bikes without tyres. For them it was a sort of a game, first to get past the Germans and secondly to see how much food they could scrounge.

It was a bike ride of about fifteen kilometres. Winter had started early and it was by then already very cold. They did their trick of shouting out 'Rosenkohl' and finally arrived at the farm. But the rumour had been false and no sprouts were available, only black salsify which they had to dig out the ground themselves. That was hard work because the ground was cold and hard but they managed to get quite a few. Then the aeroplanes came.

"Oh God, my child," my mother wailed when we could hear the aeroplanes and the bombardment.

"She could be lying dead in a field. Why did I let her go? I'll never forgive myself if anything happens to her."

"She'll be all right Mummy, she knows what to do. She will lie flat in the field as you've told her," I said trying to console her. I had never seen my mother so desperate. It frightened me and I felt helpless and had never been so sad in all of my five years.

When Dicky arrived home with the black salsify my mother hugged her while her tears of relief streamed down her face.

"Oh darling, I was so worried, what did you do? You must have been so frightened."

"We had to lie flat in the salsify field. There were some other people there. It was pretty scary but I'm all right now and when it was over we just carried on getting the salsify."

My mother cooked the long, root-like vegetables and both my mum and dad were delighted with their treat. For me it had been a very emotional day and I thought the salsify was horrid and certainly not worth all the trouble. I would have preferred a piece of sugarbeet and that was certainly not very nice of me.

The hunt for food was now never ending. Everything of value was being sold. My Aunt Bep, who's only treasure was a silver dressing-table set consisting of a silver-backed comb, brush and mirror, had become so desperate to supply food for her parents, brother and herself that she swapped it for a large bag of potatoes. All her beautiful bed linen, which she had embroidered by hand when she was engaged to be married, had gone for milk or other bits. She never did get married because her fiancé fathered a child by someone else and that was the end of the story.

Children, including my sister, would go to great lengths just to obtain a slice of bread. The risks they took were quite horrendous at times. To try and go to Rozenburg on the actual ferry became some kind of game. They would wait until the ferry would leave the quay. Just as it started to pull away they would jump on it and so cross to the island avoiding the stupid rowing boat. If they had missed they would have landed in the freezing cold water of the river and would no doubt have died. It had nothing to do with bravery or bravado; they were driven by the need to eat. My mother went nearly berserk when she heard what Dicky had been up to.

"Are you mad jumping on the ferry, you could have landed in the blooming water and what about the Germans? God only knows what might have happened."

"Mum, honestly they're used to it, kids are doing it all the time. They don't harm us. I really think they feel sort of sorry for us. Honestly, they don't even look or speak to us."

It must be said that none of the kids were ever harmed and they repeated this procedure on the other side to get home.

My sister would go from farm to farm asking for a slice of bread or some milk. When she told me about these trips she herself was still amazed at her resilience to the hardships.

"We would have to time it precisely right to jump on board, you couldn't hesitate otherwise you would have landed in the river. The Germans would just laugh and leave you alone and allow you to walk off via the gangplank. We would go to the nearest farm and ask for a slice of bread. You were often sent away and shouted at. I don't think that they had any idea how bad it was on the other side of the river. It was odd because we were totally immune to their rudeness and shouts. If we weren't given anything we'd go to the next farm. We would walk until we were given some food, sometimes just a slice of dry bread, and occasionally some milk. We would carry on until we'd had enough to eat, maybe even saving a slice for the others at home. We then had to walk back to the ferry, which was sometimes a long way. It really depended on the generosity of the farmers that day. I can understand that they got fed up with it because people came every single day without fail. They didn't have that much themselves because everything went to the Germans and they were only allowed to keep small quantities for their own use. In our eyes they had plenty though. In a way, I think, it had become a game to us, but a game grown out of desperation."

My father still received all the war information via the UK on his hidden radio. He would sit there with his headphones on and straining to catch every word. Shortly after the disaster of operation Market Garden the mood swung again.

"Mien the RAF has bombed Westkapelle, they're starting on the west side now. They've bombed one of the sea-dykes and a massive whole in the dyke is letting the water in flooding the whole island of Walcheren."

"What's so good about that? Poor people who live there."

"I'm sure they've been evacuated. The main thing is they're isolating the German troops; the Canadians are still fighting in Zeeuws Vlaanderen. They've got to get routes open to Antwerp."

"Why do they have to open up a route to Antwerp? I don't understand all this. All I'm worried about is food and how to get the house warm."

"For food supplies and all other things. If they're to start trying to cross the rivers again they need to be able to supply the troops from closer by. Not all the way from France. It's no good having Antwerp freed if you can't get into it. The Wester Schelde is full of mines so they can't use it, that means there's no way they can get from the North Sea to Antwerp."

"Oh I see, well let's hope they're successful," my mother answered. She had certainly lost her optimism and the things on her mind were certainly not the mines in the Wester Schelde.

She had more or less started to accept the situation for what it was without much hope of improvement. She was tired of the fight for survival.

The actions by the allies paid off, however, and by November 3rd they defeated the Germans in this south-westerly part of Holland and the clearing of mines could begin.

Every day my father would go to the soup kitchen, which was housed in the butcher's shop just along the road from us, to collect our pathetic meals. He was a welcome guest as he always had the latest news on how the war was going. While the man in charge was ladling the disgusting fluid into the saucepan, my dad would whisper the latest stories. The poor man was so intrigued that he sometimes lost count and quite often we were given an extra ladle or more.

One day I was allowed to go with him. Knowing about the procedures, because I had overheard my dad telling my mum, I watched carefully and when the man had finished doling out our soup I asked my father in a very loud voice:

"Dad, how many more spoonfuls did we get today?" I received such a violent clip round my ear that I nearly fell over. My father was furious.

"This stupid big mouthed little madam gave the bloody game away, didn't she? Asked in a loud voice if we'd been given a bit extra," he complained to my mother.

"Well, how was she supposed to know that it was a secret? You should have told her beforehand to keep her mouth shut."

"I didn't know she knew anything about it, did I? God you can't say anything in this house without her blurting it out. She should learn to keep her trap shut."

I was never allowed to go with him again, nor were we ever given more soup than was strictly allowed. I also never really learnt to keep my trap shut and in my primary school days I often upset the whole family by broadcasting things which should have stayed within the four walls of our house.

That wasn't completely my fault because one of the female teachers, who was a friend of my Uncle Adriaan, was very nosy and would always ask me about the family and then tell Uncle Adriaan what I had said. Much, much later, when I had left the country, my father once said to a friend that what he missed most was my big mouth.

The stricken vessel *Cornelia Clasina* after the explosion.

The whole family in front of the
shop just before we moved out.

The Canadians have arrived. My mother is on the left in the light coat and holding flowers.

Me aged eight. On the famous bridge in Maassluis.

No.11, the house I was born in, as it is now.

The shop and the little street as it is now.
My grandparents' house was the last one on the left side.
The houses at the back are all new.

11

The Hunger Winter

We were now practically starving. We had hardly any food at all, no gas, no electricity, no coal and even the water was rationed. The very, very cold weather increased the misery. All we had was a small stove to keep us warm, to cook the meagre bits of food on and to heat water.

While we were short of all the simple necessities of life the Germans were still short of manpower and transport. This brought new horrors to the already weakened and exhausted population. Massive razzias were held to round up men between eighteen and forty years old and sometimes people as old as fifty were taken. Thousands of men went into hiding, but even so approximately 50,000 were picked up in the area of Rotterdam alone and sent to work in Germany. The same happened in The Hague, Delft and surrounding areas. How much more punishment could we take?

The Germans were now plundering the country. Machinery, factory stocks and everything with wheels was taken and transported to their factories in Germany. Razzias on bicycles were held; the only transport left to us. They came with lorries and took away this precious possession, sometimes even when you were riding it, or they came and searched the house.

As always the news of these raids spread like wildfire and people quickly moved into action and hid them in places where

f

they hoped the Germans wouldn't search. Those razzias weren't done on a daily basis, so when it was over you could quite safely take the bicycle out of its hiding place again and ride it.

We had an enormous built-in cupboard in the bedroom and as soon as my mother was told they were coming to search she would take all three bikes upstairs and hide them in there behind clothes and boxes. It must have been an enormous struggle for her to get them up the narrow stairs, but she always managed.

One day, when my dad returned from work, he asked my mother if she had been able to hide the bikes in time as he had heard about the raid.

"I did and so did Peter Disaster next door," she said bursting out laughing.

"What's so funny?" my dad asked.

"Well, honestly, that man must be even more stupid than I thought he was. I was cleaning the windows outside and saw him trying to hide his bike on top of his shed's roof. A German patrolling on top of the dyke was actually watching him. But that was not the funniest part; when he had eventually managed to haul it up and was trying to put it so that it wouldn't fall off, the roof gave way and he just disappeared, bike and all." By now my mother was doubled over with laughter and so was my father.

"When I saw him later and asked if he was all right, he said, 'Yes, it was just like now you see me and now you don't.' Even the German must have found it funny because he never came for the bike nor did he look in any of the houses."

It was, of course, a tale that was told to everyone in the family and everybody had a good laugh about it. Poor Peter, we've never forgotten about him and his bike.

In the days before the war a comedian would be on the radio every week and this man had a very nasal voice. He called himself Peter Disaster. As our neighbour also had a very nasal voice and everything always went wrong for him, my mother had nicknamed him after the comedian. I don't even think his name was actually Peter. Our whole family always only referred to him by his nickname.

*   *   *   *

My sister was still constantly in search of food. She biked for miles and miles to the outlying farms, sometimes for nothing but sometimes she managed to get a bit of wheat or some vegetables.

On one of her quests she had cycled with Sjaak, one of the boys next door, to a farm along the dyke to Hook of Holland where, it was rumoured, they might be able to get some wheat. It was bitterly cold but that didn't seem to worry them much. Cycling on their crippled bikes was hard work and kept them warm.

The whispers about the wheat must have spread rapidly and when they arrived quite a few others were already there. They were all told that there was no wheat and everybody left just a little more desperate. My sister and Sjaak stayed. When lunch-time came and the family and farm workers settled themselves round the table to eat their lunch the two of them pressed their noses against the window and watched them eat.

"Go away, we have nothing to give away, we've hardly enough for ourselves," shouted the farmer's wife. But they didn't move. The farmer told them to clear off. But still they didn't move. In the end the farmer's wife came outside and said, "Please will you go away. I'll give you a slice of bread each and a bit of wheat, but then please go. It's hard for us as well, you must understand that."

Having been given a thick slice of bread and a kilo of wheat they started on their way home.

Riding high along the dyke they noticed a bike razzia in progress among the houses below. They quickly scrambled down the other side and knocked on somebody's door. An old man answered and he agreed to hide their bikes. They had to walk the rest of the way, which was about ten kilometres. When they finally arrived home they were so cold that they could hardly move.

"Oh my poor darling, you're frozen, come quick and sit by the fire. I'll get the tub out and put some more water on. God, child, did you have to walk all the way home? Why do those ignorant pigs have to have our bikes as well, they've already taken everything else?" wailed my mother.

"Will you get your bike back?" I asked her

"Yes, of course, but we'll have to walk all the way back there again to get them." I felt very sorry for her then. She looked so bedraggled, cold and close to tears and she had again brought a little bit of food for us.

The tub was placed in front of the fire; the large pan of hot water, which was constantly on the stove, poured in and my sister stepped gratefully in it. Mum quickly put some more on and stoked the fire up with some more pieces of wood. She poured the warm water all over Dicky with a jug and slowly a bit of colour crept back into her pale face.

Sometimes my mother went to the farms nearer to home to try and get some milk, mostly without success. One day, when my father was ill, she went together with my sister on their bikes. She begged and begged and finally managed to get a small bottle. My mum had told the farmer's wife that my dad was very ill and that he was in desperate need of some milk. That was a bit of a lie actually. He was poorly but it was nothing too serious, but who cared about telling a little fib if the end result was a bottle of the precious white fluid.

Over the moon they set off for home cycling along the small towpath by the canal. A chap called Minnema, who was a notorious Dutch Nazi and hated by the population of Maassluis, stopped them.

Those people loved to show their power, they could search you when they felt like it and that is precisely what he did. He found the milk and confiscated it. My mother was devastated and in tears when they arrived home.

"That swine Minnema took the little drop of milk I managed to get," she cried sitting on my father's bed. "I hope they hang the bastard when this war is over. Fat stupid pig." Tears of frustration and anger kept running down her cheeks and her language was so appalling that it frightened me. My mother hardly ever swore but now she kept shouting on and on until my father eventually managed to calm her down. There was so much hatred building up inside people and they had no way of venting it. It was like a time bomb waiting to go off.

*   *   *   *

124

"Mien, I'm really worried about Dad," my father said one day in December.

"I know, I saw him today, he just looks so tired and pale, I'm worried about him too. He just looks so worn out. Poor old soul."

"Mother said he'd stayed in bed nearly all day. He had little to eat, said he wasn't hungry. I know they have some potatoes and vegetables. Harry is still making sure that they have at least something to eat. He might be a stupid berk selling to the Germans but at least he steals enough from them to keep father and mother in food."

"Yes, that's at least something to be grateful for, I suppose."

As a matter of fact we sometimes benefited from that as well, because Grandma would give us a few potatoes or a piece of cabbage.

It was a very sad time for the family and even for me. I loved my kind granddad and didn't like him being ill. Every day we popped in to see how he was but he did not improve. He was just worn out after a life of very hard physical work. He died later in the month, aged 83.

My Uncle Adriaan told me years later how he sat with his father just before he died.

"He cried a little and I told him that he should not be afraid to die. He had been a good, hard working man who had done everything possible for his family.

" 'I'm not crying because I'm afraid, but I would like to stay a bit longer with all of you,' he had said."

After all those years tears still came into my uncle's eyes.

It was the third death in the family during wartime. My father's brother Henk died in 1942 after a long illness and Aunt Truus' husband had suddenly died in 1943. Both men had left a wife and two children.

As was custom in those days, when somebody in the family had died, the windows had to be covered with white sheets. I thought that was awfully spooky. We were used to blackout curtains at night, but white sheets in the daytime; that was really odd. It made you whisper to each other and you didn't dare laugh. On the day of the funeral everybody in the whole street covered

125

their windows with them. That was done out of respect for the family. I can't really remember much about the funeral, but it must have been a very sad episode in already very sad times.

At work my father had found out that children who had been helping a farmer to pick beans would receive a litre of milk at Christmas. He suggested that my sister should go and try to get some.

"But Dad, I didn't pick any beans, I don't know anything about it."

"I know that, but just go there and try. It's ages ago that they picked them maybe they don't remember who helped them."

"Of course they do, I'm not doing it."

"Please, just go and try. Maybe somebody won't turn up and then they might have some left. A whole litre of milk, wouldn't that be great for Christmas?"

My father did have some strange ideas I must admit, and there was no arguing against him. My mother put up a feeble protest but the thought of a whole litre of milk was very tempting and in the end she agreed that it was worth a try. She went, of course, my poor sister, and when the farmer called the name Piet Hoek and nobody stepped forward my sister did, and when the farmer said, "You're not Piet Hoek," she answered:

"No, I'm his sister," and she received the milk.

Christianity and all that it entails was not very high on the agenda that year. Morals had all but disappeared in the fight for survival. Christmas and New Year passed without much of a celebration.

The bitter cold weather stayed. Every bit of spare wood had been used. At night to get a little light my father had placed one of the bicycles on its stand in the room and my mum, dad and sister cycled in turn so the bicycle lamp, which was worked by a dynamo, gave a little glow. Candles had long been sold out. Some people had carbide lamps or little pots with some sort of oil and a wick. There were no streetlights and people used dynamo torches, which gave a tiny speck of light, but most people just stayed indoors. Occasionally we popped round to Grandma. I found that really scary because it was pitch black. Only the light of the moon, if it was visible, shed any light. I made sure I held tight to my mum's or dad's hand. We had to do that before eight o'clock of course, because we all had to be in by then.

To keep warm everybody went to bed very early, but sleep was not always possible because they were so hungry. People were dying in the streets, even in our little town. They were found with swollen bellies. One of my mother's uncles died this horrible death.

It was then that my father had the idea of sending my sister on her trip to Zwartewaal. A lot of harsh words were said before my mother would let her go. My sister was very frightened because for the first time she could not take a friend for support. She had to make this journey all on her own to a place she had never been to but she nevertheless agreed to go.

"I'm scared Dad, because I always go with somebody else, what if I can't find it?"

"I know exactly where it is, so I will tell you how to get there. It's easier now you're going on the small boat instead of the rowing boat because you'll be dropped on Voorne itself. I know where the landing place is and I'll tell you exactly how to get to Zwartewaal from there. Don't be afraid, you'll be all right, I promise. If I thought you would be in any danger I wouldn't ask you to go."

"How far is it? Can I come back the same day?"

"No lass, you'll have to stay the night. It's too far for doing it in one day and you might have to wait a while before you can cross the river in that rowing boat on the way back."

"What if they won't let her in the house? What if she has to stay outdoors all night? Have you thought about that?" my mother screamed.

"Don't be stupid woman, of course they won't let her stay outside."

"How the hell do you know that?"

"Because nobody in their right mind would leave a little girl standing on the step and certainly no relation of mine would ever dream of doing that."

And so she went.

The next day my mother's sister, Aunt Dit, had cycled from Vlaardingen in search of food at the farms which lie along a narrow country road from Vlaardingen to Maassluis. She'd had no luck and came over to see us. When she heard the story of my sister's trip and saw how distressed and worried my mother was, she decided to stay and wait. I always loved it when she visited, because she was such fun. Even now she managed to make my mother laugh.

"Have you still got any wood, Mien?"

"We've got a bit and some coal. Kardien found some by the power station. Hundreds of people are trying to find some there. It's all gone now, of course."

"Well, I've burned our bed. Good solid wood it was, you know. Burned for ages."

"You did what?" asked my mother.

"I burned my bed, we're sleeping on the mattress on the floor now."

Despite their miseries, they both burst out laughing.

"What ever did Gerrit say?"

"He couldn't say much, could he? I had nothing else to put on the fire and he is in no hurry to try and get some, so it was the bed or nothing."

"What are you burning next, though?"

"I've managed to get some more wood now. But people are burning the floor boards out of their living-rooms and living in the kitchen, you know."

"Yes, I've heard that and you know the tram lines in Rotterdam, well, people are getting the little blocks of wood which sit in the middle of the lines out. I can count myself lucky. Kardien and his mates have stolen some old railway sleepers. Blooming dangerous business mind to get them. They have to do it in the middle of the night and they have to cut them up first, of course, before they can bring them home. They know at what times the Krauts patrol the area, they lie in wait and as soon as the soldiers have gone they move in. If they get caught they'll be shot there and then."

"How do they get it home, though?"

"I think they push them over the embankment, well out of the way of the patrols, cut them up and then tie them onto their bikes. I don't ask too much. I'm just pleased when he gets home in one piece. God, Dit, when is this ever going to end? Still, I suppose we've got to count ourselves lucky, we're still together and alive. Like another cup of this revolting surrogate coffee?"

I had been playing with the few toys I had but my ears had been wide open. How could you burn your bed? I couldn't imagine having to sleep on the floor. It was bad enough to lie on the floor when we were being bombed. Maybe she would burn the table and chairs next and then they would all have to sit on the floor and eat their food from the carpet, like having a picnic. My aunt was certainly mad in my eyes. Nevertheless I was pleased she'd come because it had taken the stress out of the situation.

And then at last my father returned with my sister. My mother ran to the door and burst into tears. She dragged my sister in and put her straight by the fire where she was also hugged tightly by my aunt. My father, who was also obviously relieved that she had returned safely, was left putting the bike away and taking care of the food. That he was also frozen solid from waiting for her for hours was of no importance to my mother. Even I was relieved to see her back.

When the whole story of her ordeal unfolded this brave little girl was quite a hero to me. The next day it all had to be told again to my grandmother.

When all the goodies were viewed, the little piece of bacon was placed in the middle of the table. We held hands and danced around it singing and laughing. Such was the happiness we felt, just because we had a little piece of meat. My aunt had to go then, because everybody had to be in by eight o'clock and it took her at least half an hour to cycle home on her bike with wooden tyres. She didn't go home empty-handed, of course. My sister had made us all very happy.

A few days later my father managed to retrieve the potatoes.

Mrs Sluyter, the woman from a few houses further on, the one who had the baby, came to the door and said, "Mrs Hoek, I've heard you have some potatoes. If you peel them, please can I have the peels?"

My mother, who probably had no intention of peeling them, felt terrible about it but agreed. She scrubbed them first and then peeled them rather carelessly, so some goodness was still left on them and she also gave her a few whole ones. When my mum went to bring them to her, she was very, very grateful and she thanked my mum over and over again. That's how bad the situation was.

The old and the small were, as always, the most vulnerable. Babies and small children were crying in their cots. Starving mothers' breasts were dry. More than fifteen thousand people died of hunger, often reduced to mere skeletons. Tens of thousands more suffered from hunger oedema. Sick people had to be transported to hospitals on handcarts. The dead could not be buried; there was no wood for coffins and the ground was frozen solid. In the end they were buried in cardboard boxes.

My mother became thinner and thinner, saving the food for us and taking herself as little as possible. The bones in her already naturally pinched face began to stand out more and more and her nose seemed to grow longer and longer. There was no party for my sixth birthday.

12

Light at the End of the Tunnel

The railway line from Rotterdam to Hook of Holland runs through Maassluis past the large housing estate at The Head and further on divides the outer harbour from the inner harbour. The Germans, who were now the only ones using the trains, were petrified of sabotage. They had, therefore, built a huge fence from rejected railway sleepers so nobody could get onto the lines. The actual railway station was on the other side of the lines and soldiers always guarded the entrance to that.

At the height of this ongoing freezing weather when desperation overtook reason, a large crowd of men from this estate, including my Uncle Arie, got together and devised a plan to secure a large amount of firewood.

It had to be very secretive because spies were everywhere. One night they crept with little sledges to this enormous fence and demolished it completely in one go. Snow was still on the ground and the massive sleepers were transported on the sledges that had been tied together. That they weren't caught was nothing short of a miracle.

It became the talk of the town and everybody went to have a look at where the fence had once been. It was a feat which nobody could ever have thought feasible, but they did it. The town cheered. My father loved the story, even more so because his brother had been involved. We, of course, also went to have a look at this site of great achievement. It became a monument of bravery to us and of ridicule to the Germans. It was an acute embarrassment for them.

"God knows how they did it. Arie might tell us one day but at the moment everybody keeps mum. I wonder where they stored it all. Blimey Mien, what a great job and what a poke in the eye for those bloody Krauts," my father said proudly as if he had been involved himself.

"Absolutely, they did a brilliant job. I only hope that the Germans won't take revenge because, if they do, God help us. I am rather worried about that actually. What do you think, will they retaliate?"

"Wouldn't think so, they would have to shoot the whole town. I think their guards will be punished though. Somebody will have to take the blame for letting this happen and, by the way, don't mention to anybody that Arie was involved, the less people know the better."

"No, don't worry, I shan't say a word."

No retribution followed, or at least not on the population of Maassluis. For a while there were many bright fires in the houses of the estate though.

Our little world had become a very bleak place. Trees had all but disappeared; wooden gates or railings had been demolished, either by their owners or by another poor soul. Other targets were empty houses. Doors, floorboards and everything else that would burn were taken from them.

The nights were spookier than ever. The town resembled a scene out of a horror story; everything was black with even blacker shapes rising out of the doom. All windows were tightly covered with blackout curtains. What the use of that was I don't know as we had hardly any light in the houses in any case. The only good thing about all this darkness was that people could sneak out in the middle of the night to try and steal some wood or coal.

My father had heard that one lot of Germans, who inhabited one of the posh houses on the estate on top of the dyke, had left. He knew that there was wood and coal in the garden. He had seen

132

it when he had walked passed there and it had made him cross that they had everything and we had nothing.

The house was right on the corner, so entrance to the garden was simple. One night he decided to go and help himself. All was dark and quiet when he got there and he started to fill a sack with wood and some coal. Then he heard voices and laughter and saw some of the patrols returning from their duties and enter the house which was supposed to be empty. He nearly died on the spot with fear. He crouched behind the bushes and sat there for so long that he nearly froze to death.

After what seemed hours to him, the soldiers must have gone to bed because everything went quiet again and he made his way home with his sack of fuel.

The risks of doing such things were high. If you were caught being outside, let alone stealing from the Germans, you might be shot or, at best, sent to a concentration camp.

Apart from food and fuel to stay warm, clothes became a big problem. Everything was threadbare and worn out. Shoes were no longer available. Some people wore pieces of wood strapped to their feet by whatever means they could think of.

By January rations had gone down to 500 grams of bread per person per week and half a litre of soup per day, the soup having no nourishment in it at all. We sometimes had a bit of porridge, which was just flour cooked in water, and other tiny helpings of whatever my sister had managed to find. To try and make the most of what was available, recipes were distributed on how to make porridge from sugarbeets or how to fry tulip bulbs and make soup from dahlia tubers.

A lot of people made syrup from sugarbeets. The beets were cut into small pieces and boiled into a mash with a little bit of water. The whole lot was then sieved and put back on the fire. When all the liquid had evaporated a sweet tasting syrup remained. My mother did this quite often. One evening she had put the mash back on the stove and put a little bit of very inferior coal on the fire. Unfortunately the coal was so bad it wouldn't light and the fire went out. They decided to go to bed instead and light the stove again in the morning, leaving the pan where it was.

Unbeknown to them the stove had very slowly come to life again and when they woke up the next morning and went downstairs everything was black. The mash had burned to a cinder and black clouds of smoke hung everywhere. The fire was still burning. We coughed and spluttered and all the windows and doors had to be opened until we could breathe again. The saucepan had to go in the bin and it took my mum ages and ages to clean the walls, windows and paintwork. She never left anything, apart from water, on the fire again. The worst thing was not that everything was filthy, however, but that we had no syrup and no more sugarbeets to make more.

Our shop was often closed now, because we had so little to sell, but one afternoon there was a knock on the door. My mother went to open it and found one of the reps, who in better times had come to take orders, on the doorstep. He was so thin that my mum hardly recognised him. He asked her if we please had something for him to eat. All we had in the house at that time was a little flour.

My mum, well aware that this was all we had, went nevertheless to the kitchen, put the flour and water into a saucepan and cooked it on the stove in the living-room. When it was ready she put the saucepan on the table in front of him. My sister and I sat on the opposite side of the table and watched him eat the very last bit of our food. The porridge was a little burned and we hoped he would leave these bits, so that the two of us could share them. He ate everything though; scraping the bottom so clean that washing the pan was hardly necessary.

My sister and I sat in stunned silence, not understanding why our mother had given away our last tiny bit of food.

With tears in his eyes he thanked my mother and he told us that he had come all the way from Rotterdam to try and find something to eat for his family. He had walked all the way and was so weak and hungry that in total desperation he had called on us. We knew then that other people were even worse off than us and we forgave our mum for her generosity.

It became one of the most vivid images of that terrible winter for me and I have never forgotten that desperate person.

Trying to get food was now the main occupation of the people. For children it was, sometimes, also a game.

It was normal practice in Holland that when the canals were frozen over, holes were hacked in the ice so that the coots had somewhere to swim. That was no different this winter. Young boys would go to these holes with long sticks with nails on the end. The game was to bang the sticks on the ice to frighten the coots and then when they flew up to catch them by spearing them onto the nails. It was awfully cruel but starvation made people do things they would normally never have dreamed of. We never ate them, nor did we ever eat tulip bulbs, but many people around us did.

More people had been picked up in Maassluis and sent away to serve the Germans. They were now also short of people at the front and some of those who were picked up in the later stages of the war were to train for warfare, which was a total fiasco because the Dutch people pretended not to understand their master and did everything wrong on purpose. They were ordered to wear German military uniforms; if they refused they were sent to concentration camps.

Some of this training was done in Czechoslovakia near the Russian front.

When it became clear that the Russians were getting closer and closer the Germans got scared and they left in great haste with some of the more willing people to walk back to Germany. The ones left behind, amongst them some of the people from Maassluis, were taken prisoner by the Russians and put into concentration camps.

The problem was that they were still wearing their uniforms, so the Russians thought they were Germans and they were treated very, very badly. They tried to explain that they were not Germans but nobody understood them and they had no means of proving it until an interpreter eventually arrived and explained that they were Dutch and had been forced to wear those clothes. Every single one of those people suffered greatly but most of them returned safely when the war was over. However, they were often mentally scarred for life.

Despite the misery of our existence, humour was never very far away in our house. We had been to visit Aunt Lien, my mother's brother Dirk's wife. She found life very difficult trying to cope with her three children while her husband was somewhere serving with the English Navy. Very little was heard from their men, just sometimes a small note saying that they were all right. These were sent through the Red Cross but couldn't contain more than twenty-five words and that included the address.

My aunt was a perpetual moaner at the best of times and in a complaining voice she told us the story of the accident the boys had had with the soup from the communal kitchen. My mother commiserated with her but, however awful it was, it had tickled her no end.

"I went to see Lien today," she told my dad.

"Oh, how is she, coping all right?"

"Of course she's not coping, does nothing but moan, mind, it can't be easy for her I suppose, mustn't be too hard on her. She told me such a funny story though, well not funny to her but I couldn't help laughing. She sent the two boys to the soup kitchen and as always put it in the bowls as soon as they came in, hoping it would still be a bit warm. She thought that there wasn't very much and that it looked even more watery than ever, but she didn't take that much notice; just presumed that the rations had been lowered again. When she was eating it she thought it tasted very odd, a bit as if she was eating sand or dirt. She asked the boys if they tasted anything strange. No, it tasted fine to them, they said. Lien noticed that they had both gone bright red, so she asked them why they were blushing. Had they something to confess by any chance? It turned out that they had dropped the saucepan, spilled part of it and then tried to recoup it from the street, dirt, grime and all and then put some water in it to make it look a bit more."

When my mother finished telling the story to my dad they were both in fits of laughter.

"Oh, God, poor Lien, how revolting. Those poor boys must have been petrified when they dropped it," my father said, trying to be serious again.

"Well, they were. Poor lads didn't know what to do. Problem was they had nothing else to eat so they just had to swallow it. I shouldn't laugh about it really, but it was the way she was telling it. I could just imagine those two little boys trying to scrape soup from the cobble stones."

Our plight was by now known throughout Europe and at the end of January 1945 a ship filled with food and medicine arrived from Sweden in Delfzijl, a port in the North of the country. The Germans had given permission for this cargo to be transferred to barges and to be transported via the IJsselmeer to the West of the country. We didn't see much, if any, of this first shipment because the IJsselmeer is a long way away from us and the railways couldn't be used because they were now only for the Germans. There was little transport on the roads because the enemy had confiscated all cars and vans, and the canals were all still frozen.

England was one of the countries which wanted desperately to help us. As transport by ship was still out of the question because of mines they began to think of dropping food from aeroplanes. They started to experiment. The British Bomber Command began to sort out the technical details but the correct procedures of packing the food and how to drop it had yet to be worked out.

On February 24th 1945 a four-engined Lancaster bomber from the 115th squadron at Witchford went to Netheravon for experiments. In those days nobody knew exactly how to go about it and a lot of practice was necessary. It took until the end of April before the first aeroplanes took off. The Germans had reluctantly agreed to the drops.

On April 29th at twelve o'clock Radio Oranje broadcast that the first Lancasters had taken to the skies. Every aeroplane carried five bundles wrapped in sailcloth each containing seventy sacks of food. The contents were flour, powdered egg, peas, beans, tins of meat and vegetables, tea, sugar, chocolate and other necessities. They dropped it at pre-agreed places such as the airfields Schiphol, Waalhaven and Ypenburg but also at other places so that distribution was easy. Everybody in Maassluis was outside. I clearly remember the wonderful site of low flying aeroplanes coming in over the Waterway en route to The Hague. Everybody was waving and shouting at them. Operation 'Manna' had well and truly started.

The Americans came into action on May 1st with their Flying Forts. Nearly 400 four-engined Boeing B-17s dropped their manna near The Hague and Rotterdam. The next day 400 Flying Forts and 500 Lancasters took to the sky. Every day aeroplanes came over and the best was we didn't have to be afraid of them. The last of the aeroplanes took off on May 8th. It had been a magnificent operation. The Americans made a total of 2,200 flights and the RAF more than 3,150. The total amount of food they dropped was estimated at 11,785 metric tonnes.

It emerged much later that many pilots had volunteered for this operation. To them it was a way of saying thank you to the Dutch population who had helped many English pilots, who had been shot down over our country, to stay out of the hands of the Germans. At the first opportunity they were smuggled back to England, their helpers often risking their own lives.

Just to know that people were thinking about us and were trying so hard to help us brought hope back into our lives. From the time we knew that Sweden was sending food we again believed that the end was in sight, that there was indeed light at the end of the tunnel.

This was all such good news because we knew that our rations would soon improve and that some proper food would again be filling our bellies. But big clouds were still overshadowing our delight because terrible things were still happening.

The allies once again bombed The Hague at the beginning of March. Their aim was to destroy German rocket launchers but instead hundreds of innocent people were killed.

A few days after this terrible disaster the population received again some fantastic news and hope returned that soon our country would once more belong to us.

Running into the shop, hardly giving himself time to shut the door behind him, my father shouted, "Mien, have you heard? Queen Wilhelmina is back in the country. Now we know for sure it will be over soon. She's in the South, of course, but she must know even more than what Radio Oranje tells us, she must know that the Germans are on their last legs."

"Is she? Is she really? That's brilliant. It's the best news for five whole years. God I wished we were allowed the put the flag out," answered my mother. They were so delighted that I wouldn't have been surprised if they had started to sing Wilhelmus van Nassau, our national anthem.

I'd heard about the Queen, of course, and Prince Bernard and I suppose I was pleased that my parents were so delighted. I was actually far more pleased that the weather was changing and that I could play outside again.

Life had become quite dull really. We still visited family and Grandma of course, but there were never nice treats now. Playing with my little friends was quite often boring because we had so little to play with. That we were all very weak and tired through lack of food never occurred to me.

I sometimes envied my sister because she could go on all those cycling trips, even though it was mainly to go and look for food. It was not until many years later that I understood how hard it had been for her. How often she had cycled miles in freezing weather in threadbare clothes and had come back empty handed.

My father's good mood continued because the news he was still receiving on his illegal radio was encouraging. Every time a town was freed or advances were made by the allies he would repeat to us what he had just heard and then go out, mostly first to his mother. More and more towns were being liberated and when on March 22nd the allies crossed the Rhine his relief and happiness was complete.

"Yes, Mien they've done it, they've bloody done it, they've crossed the Rhine, they're nearly here, must go and tell mother and Bep." I was still sent out with messages sometimes, but not as often as when I was smaller. I don't know why exactly, but maybe I was now too old to have messages pinned to my vest. Shame really because I felt quite important doing that.

On May 4th Grandma celebrated her birthday once more. The news had been that our liberation was imminent. We went to

Grandma in the early evening and some of the other relations had also arrived. All the talk was of the German defeat. Encouraged by the sheer thought of regaining our freedom some of my uncles and my dad went outside even though it was after eight o'clock. Other people were in the streets already celebrating. Then we heard shots and they came running back in. The Germans had opened fire. We were obviously still at war. Nobody was hurt but the danger still existed.

After all was quiet we crept back home. Straight after we got back my father put on his headphones to listen to the latest news and again it was stated that the Germans were about to capitulate.

The following day something else happened which made us even more certain that the war was on its last legs. Two English vessels, crammed full of food, came sailing up the New Waterway on their way to Rotterdam. A German war ship was escorting them so that a mine wouldn't blow them out the water.

One of the inhabitants of Maassluis, a Mr Martien van der Hidde, had been told about this little convoy the previous day. He was very keen to express his thanks to the seamen and the English in general. He immediately set to work and managed to have a wooden frame made with a diameter of 2.3 metres.

Flowers had been available all through the war years, however strange this might seem, and many a house was cheered up with a small bunch of brightly coloured blooms. He had, therefore, no problem in ordering the florist to cover this frame in flowers. A large Dutch flag was draped in the middle of the arrangement and on the white part was written 'MAASSLUIS DANKT DEN ZEEMAN' (Maassluis says thank you to the seaman).

He kept all his plans secret because we were still occupied. When he knew the vessels had entered Hook of Holland he transported it to The Head and loaded it onto a small tug.

By now a large part of the population of Maassluis had heard about it and everybody still able to walk went to The Head. They waved to the small tug when it set off for its rendezvous. When this small boat passed the German escort vessel they noticed many officers on the bridge nervously looking through their binoculars.

140

When they reached the first English vessel, the MS *Lesto*, a German liaison officer, who was on board, started shouting and told them to clear off. But Mr van der Hidde spoke English and asked for the captain to come to the rail. Captain Culbertson willingly obliged and when he was asked to accept the floral tribute in the name of all the people of Maassluis, he was delighted to do so.

The German liaison officer kept shouting and forbade them to hand over the flowers but nobody took any notice of him. When the *Lesto* and *Empire Scout* sailed passed the harbour in Maassluis the flowers were clearly visible and the population waved, shouted and clapped their hands in welcome.

A few days later Mr van der Hidde invited the two captains and another couple of the crew members to visit Maassluis. It had been decided that they would have a meal in his house. He had been offered some slightly better ingredients to prepare a meal for them but he decided that it would be more fitting if they ate the same food as we had had to eat during the last six months, which was the soup from the communal kitchen and the foul black bread. The only difference being that they were offered two slices of bread instead of our normal ration of just one. Being English they politely declared that 'it hadn't tasted too badly'.

On the same day of these vessels sailing into Rotterdam, Saturday May 5th 1945, the papers for our freedom were signed in a hotel appropriately called 'De Wereld' (The World). The Germans capitulated. Prince Bernhard, a German himself, attended the ceremony.

13

The Aftermath

On paper we were free but the reality was somewhat different. The Germans were still everywhere. Their frustration and disbelief that they had lost the war made them even more dangerous. The population, drunk with happiness, dared taunting them, which sometimes had terrible results.

In Vlaardingen a group of young men were celebrating near the harbour. One of them was a relation of my father's sister. They were laughing and joking and poking fun at a German. Without so much as a warning the soldier pulled his pistol and shot him dead.

On May 7th the population of Amsterdam was celebrating at the Dam. They were dancing and singing, just showing their happiness and relief when the Germans, again without any warning, opened fire. Some people were killed, others wounded. Fear returned. All we could do now was wait for the allies to come to rid us of our oppressors and drive them out of our lives for good.

And on May 8th 1945, on this wonderful day, they came. From the early morning onwards rumours were flying that they would be in Maassluis before lunch-time. People were buying flowers in anticipation of their arrival. The town had once more come alive. Everybody was talking to everybody. People had put on their best clothes; their gaunt and tired faces beaming with delight.

We had been told that the Canadians were on their way from Delft, driving their tanks through the villages to Maassluis, where they would be stationed in the carpet factory where my father worked. Everybody was out on the streets. Some had brought our beloved red, white and blue flags, which we hadn't been allowed to show for five whole years.

By 10.30 people were shouting, "They've arrived in Maasland," which is only a few miles away. People flocked to the road which leads to this village. The market place was a heaving mass of jubilant people. The progress of our saviours to our town was shouted out every few minutes. And then they were there. Smiling and waving Canadians, their tanks bedecked with flowers and young girls. People were screaming, laughing and crying all at the same time. It was an emotion that cannot be described. Only the people who experienced it know what it felt like. I was only six years old but I have never forgotten this moment of supreme relief and happiness. It was tangible. People were hugging each other, singing, dancing and shouting and for a while hunger was completely forgotten.

At night everybody was partying; well, not everybody, I wasn't allowed out, of course. My sister had gone off with her friends but I was deemed too small. I was furious.

"I want to go out as well, I'm never allowed to do anything. That stupid girl is always allowed to do everything she wants," I shouted at my mother.

"Darling we've been out all day, you're too small to go out on your own."

"So why don't you come with me then?"

"Because it's your bedtime, we'll go out again tomorrow."

"Well, it's not fair. I've got to go to bed while she's allowed to go lurching around with boys." That made my mother laugh so much that despite my misery I had to laugh as well. The 'lurching around with boys' became an idiom in our family and we still use it today.

After the elation came the reckoning. Five years of pent-up

frustration and anger released itself in the most horrific deeds. It was terrible and cruel.

People who had been known for their German sympathies were dragged from their houses and beaten, sometimes through the whole of the town with the people cheering and calling them names. Not very far from where we lived a man was dragged away, his wife screaming as she tried to prevent them from taking him.

Those incidents were so bad that my mother would take me back inside and she herself would stay indoors because she was not able to watch such cruelty.

She despised all people who had sided with the Germans but still did not believe that people should take the law into their own hands. It was a sad but understandable fact that, in some cases, even the mildest people turned into savages.

When my mother was very young she was in service by a family called Franke. My mother liked the lady very much but her husband was a terrible man. He used to beat his wife and the children had to call him Majesty Pa. My mother didn't just hate him she loathed him. Typical for such a type of person, he had joined the German ranks and had betrayed many Jews in the town who were taken away never to be seen again. He had been one of the worst, if not the worst traitor in the whole town. He was taken from his house and beaten to death by those people who had suffered and were crazed with anger. That was the only time that my mother agreed with the rule of the mob.

"You know I don't agree with a lot that's going on at the moment but I'm pleased that they killed that swine Franke. I would have pleasantly watched him getting his come-uppance. If there ever was a man who deserved it, it was him, and not only for what he did in the war but for what he did to his poor wife and children. He must have been one of the lowest of human beings I've ever come across in my life," she told my dad.

My Aunt Nel's husband, Harry, was jailed for six months for selling to the Germans. That created a bit of a stir in the family.

"Mother is really upset about Harry, you know, they just came to the house and took him away. It's a terrible shock for Nel," my father said after a visit to his mother.

"Well he shouldn't have done it then should he? They even had Germans visiting them sometimes; you know that as well as I do. It has always been swept under the carpet by the whole family and now he's got what he deserves," retorted my mother.

"Yes, I know, but he was good to mother and father and we did benefit from it sometimes."

"I know that Kardien, but that doesn't take away the fact that he was rather friendly with the Krauts. No, I'm sorry, he had it coming to him."

"Another thing is that Wim Mooiman is one of his guards and now Nel won't speak to Jan and Anna."

"That's blooming stupid, Wim is only Jan and Anna's son-in-law for goodness sake, and anyway Wim didn't put him there himself, did he? God, how pathetic can you get to take it out on them? That's great for your mother and Bep isn't it. What are they supposed to do, not speak to them either, or hold two separate birthday parties, or tell them what time they're allowed to visit? Jesus, we've just been freed and already families are not talking to each other. I can't believe I'm hearing this. Look, I feel sorry for Nel in a way and even more so for the girls, but they've made a lot of money during those five years so six months in jail isn't that much of a disaster, is it?"

"No, maybe you're right, but don't argue your point too much when you see mother."

"I'll try, but I'm not going to sympathise with Harry and that's for sure."

The anger of the population of Maassluis was also directed at the women who had had affairs with the Germans. They were all picked up from their houses, including my aunt, the wife of my mother's youngest brother. They had their heads shaved and afterwards were paraded through the town on a horse and cart. It was a dreadful sight. Many were in tears, bowing their bald heads, which looked red and sore, but the people did not feel pity for them. They were shouting abuse and waving their fists. It was very degrading and although my parents were in full agreement with the fact that they should be punished, they thought that the

g

shaving of their heads was a bit over the top. To me it was the oddest thing I'd ever seen and I stood looking with my mouth wide open, even forgetting to suck my thumb.

Aunt Lena, who was the aunt in question, was married to my mother's youngest brother, Tienus. Their marriage was in trouble well before the war started and apart from the two daughters she had with my uncle, she now had a son by a German. My mother had never liked her and after she had seen her going to the cinema on the arm of a German, she had never spoken to her again. The birth of the child had rubbed more salt in the wound. The father of this child disappeared after the war never to be heard of again.

My mother adored her brother and hoped he would divorce her as soon as he came back. Adultery was a grave sin in my mother's book and him going back to her and her German son was certainly not an option.

As it happened his ship, a mine-sweeper, was the first one to sail into Rotterdam after the war. It soon became apparent that he hadn't been an angel either while serving with the English Navy as he now had a little daughter by an English woman. The difference was, of course, she wasn't the enemy.

The Germans had left the country. Seyss-Inquart, our ruler, had been taken away by the Canadians. We saw hundreds and hundreds of soldiers walking on top of the dyke on their way to Rotterdam. They were a sorry sight. Tired from their long walk from Hook of Holland, having been spat at and had abuse shouted at them along the way, they looked bedraggled, totally defeated and thoroughly fed up. I suppose many of them were just as pleased that it was all over as we were.

However much we hated them all, not every German was a bad person. Some were decent people with families back home. They would have liked it much better if they could have stayed at home with them but they were given no choice. Most of them had been ordered to join this useless war.

"I felt a bit sorry for them, they looked so terrible," my mother told my dad. "There were hundreds of them, they all looked unwashed and scruffy, nothing like the posh leather booted pigs we've been used to."

"Well, it must be hard on them, they never believed they would lose, did they? Now they have to slink off with their tail between their legs. Bloody good job, too. Bastards. Sorry but I can't feel sorry for them. Just keep bearing in mind what they've done to us Mien. They can all drop dead as far as I'm concerned."

More and more people returned from Germany where they had either been forced to work or detained in concentration camps. They were the lucky ones. More than 230,000 Dutch people lost their lives. Fifteen thousand alone died in the west of the country during the hunger winter. Thousands upon thousands of Jews never returned from the camps. Many seamen, sailing on our war ships, tugs and whatever other vessels taking part in the war, died. Thousands of innocent people were killed during bombardments by the Germans and the allies and thousands more were executed by the Nazis for being in the resistance or just because they were in the wrong place at the wrong time. Many perished in concentration camps. We were lucky; we had only lost loved ones through natural causes.

Had it not been for the organisations that looked after people in hiding, the toll would have been even greater. They looked after some 40,000 people, including about 20,000 Jews. They made sure they had money, food and clothing. Those people were the unsung heroes, risking their own lives time and time again for the sake of their fellow Dutchmen and for the stranded allied pilots.

Thousands of houses had been destroyed, first by the bombings of the Germans and later by the allies. The heart of Rotterdam was one big ruin. The harbours were practically useless. Our own little town was littered with bombed houses, churches and shops. But we were free and alive.

Uncle Jo returned from Germany. Big parties were held in every street where one of the loved ones returned. Much to my mother's relief her three brothers returned home safely.

Uncle Tienus managed to come and see us very soon after he had sailed into Rotterdam. At that time we were still eating soup from the communal kitchens and the foul black bread. He arrived when we were just having our meal. With tears in his eyes he watched us eat our meagre rations. He couldn't believe that that was all we had. He promised to bring us some better food from aboard ship the next day. We couldn't wait.

He came carrying a large dish full of appetising mashed potatoes and corned beef plus some fat to melt and put through it. My mother heated it up on the stove and then we sat down and ate the lot in one go nearly licking the dish out as well. What luxury! I had never tasted anything so luscious in all my life. Again my uncle watched us eat, pity showing on his face. He told us later that he heard that it was bad in the west of the country but he had not realised how bad it really was.

At night my mother became very ill. She was violently sick and had the most terrible pains in her stomach. She was crying and more or less crawling on the floor with pain. We were all very worried, but after a few hours it wore off and the next day she felt much better again. Much later it turned out she had gallstones and the delicious, nutritious food and the fat had brought on this horrible attack.

When all the hated German ships had left our harbour, English and American ships took their places. These became the main attraction in the town and young girls, including my sister, would go to the quayside and beg for chocolate or chewing gum. The soldiers were kind and handed it out freely.

I tried my luck once but apart from nearly being pushed into the harbour by the throng, I didn't get anything. I was obviously far too small to be noticed. Totally disillusioned with those men, who only had eyes for the big girls, I returned home. I never tried again. My sister became the provider once more, always saving a small piece of chocolate or chewing gum for me. I had never tasted anything so wonderful than this first piece of chocolate, while the chewing gum was retained in my mouth for hours on end.

Very slowly the distribution of food got under way. Transport was still bad but deliveries were made to a few central shops and the first things available were bread and biscuits. Long queues formed and you sometimes had to wait for hours to be served. Nobody minded that because at the end of the wait there was the beautiful white bread, which we called Swedish bread, presumably because it had been baked with flour from Sweden. Wheat biscuits were distributed in tins and now, when we visited Grandma, Aunt Bep would get the tin out and would give me one as a very special treat. However, I had never consciously known, or noticed the absence of, such delicacies. I had to admit that the taste was much better than sugarbeets and the foul soup from the communal kitchen.

My mother started to lose her haggard and worried look now she could feed us some proper food once more. I think that mothers suffered the most in this dreadful hunger winter; starving themselves to feed the little there was to their family. Mothers saw their babies die either from hunger or cold. They saw their lethargic and underfed children wasting away. They could not even keep them warm or clothe them properly and there was nothing they could do.

Schools started again. Life was still very basic. We still couldn't buy any clothes or shoes and needed coupons for absolutely everything but at least we were no longer starving. We could go visiting at night again. Many people took a walk to The Head in the evening where our own tugs, returning from the war, started to fill the harbour once more. The *Blankenburg* arrived first on May 8th, followed by the *Dexterous* on June 8th, which had played a big part in the towing of the *Phoenix Caissons* to the Isle of Wight. The last one, the *Witte Zee* returned on December 24th. In all twelve came back. Some were lost forever.

A few of the men who had been away with their ships during the five years returned to find their wives with a shaven head. The shock to them was immense. My father knew one of them. This man forgave his young wife and begged my dad to lend him some money to buy her a wig. We didn't have much money but both my parents reluctantly agreed to help him because they felt sorry for him. He faithfully promised to pay it back as soon as he could. Unfortunately this never happened. My parents felt utterly betrayed and my father never spoke to him again.

Trains started to run normally again. Electricity and gas supplies were restored, water was again available twenty-four hours a day and very slowly stock came back into our shop. Now the food, which was grown all around us, was for us to eat and no longer seized by the Germans. Life started to return to normal.

On October 1st 1946 Arthur Seyss-Inquart, our ruler and oppressor for five whole years, was hanged in Nuremberg. He was accused and found guilty of crimes against the peace, war crimes and crimes against humanity. He was fifty-four years old.

14

Back to Normality

I went back to nursery school and yet again loved it. Life was so
much easier now. No threats of bombings, no lying flat on your
stomach under the table or in the alcove. I started to realise what
peace meant. All the horrors, to which I had been accustomed in
my short life, had never really bothered me that much because I
was used to them, but now I understood how much better it all
was. No more whispering in the street. No more worries about
how many people were seen together talking to each other. No
more secretive listening to the radio. No more blackout curtains,
but above all no more intimidating Germans marching through
the streets.

Food was still very scarce but what we had was tasty and
nutritious. Anything was better than the foul soup and black
bread.

Summer arrived and in June my sister celebrated her thirteenth
birthday. For her the change from war to peace was rather
dramatic. She was now back at school and the quests for food
were no longer necessary. For her it was quite dull in a way now
life was back to a more regular timetable, because despite all the
hardships she had had to endure on her journeys, it had also been
a big adventure.

Apart from sending us food Sweden had also organised for a
lot of children to be sent there for a few weeks so they could be

fed properly and recoup their strength. You could apply for that and obviously my mum put my sister on the list. The youngsters were weighed and measured. Only the very weakest were chosen. I was too young in any case but my sister didn't qualify either, which was a shame really because she'd done so much for us and she really wanted to go. We were all very disappointed but I think, if the truth were known, my mum was quite relieved. She would never have stopped worrying about her.

One of the neighbouring girls was chosen but unfortunately she was quite a shy girl and she was in a state of total panic that she had to leave her family. She cried for days and begged her mum not to let her go, but she was eventually persuaded that it was for her own good and off she went. She came back looking healthy and strong, although the experience had been quite traumatic for her and it took her a long time to get over her ordeal.

It must have been rather difficult for these poor children, already worn out after that terrible winter, then to be placed with strangers whose language they did not speak and whose customs they did not know.

I was just happy to be able to run around and play outside with the only hazard being the occasional horse and cart driving along our small road. We played games again with our marbles or skipped with far more energy now that our stomachs were full. We went for walks, picked daisies and made chains.

Sitting outside on the pavement on an old blanket we made metres of French knitting from old scraps of wool. We didn't have the proper gear, of course, but we used an empty cotton reel in which our mothers had hammered four little nails and we used a large darning needle to put the loops over the nails.

We played bridegroom and bride and I was always the bride, because my grandma allowed me to pick some flowers out of her garden for my bouquet. Well, that's my account but if I'm honest it was more like: 'If I can't be the bride, I won't play'.

Old net curtains were used to make veils and old skirts or dresses dug out of our mothers' wardrobes were secured with safety pins to make the gowns of the bride and the party-goers. The groom, who was also a girl because boys thought we were

152

just silly and wouldn't play with us, always wore some kind of trousers and a jacket, which was either far too small or far too big, and a hat of some sort. We would go through the streets of the estate until we got fed up with it and we had to think of something else to do. We were always outside and the days were warm and sunny, but I'm sure that's just an illusion and it must have rained sometimes.

On weekends, when tyres became available again, we went out on the bicycles, me still sitting in a little seat on the back of my Dad's or Mum's bike, and when the beaches were cleared of mines we could once more go to the seaside. Life was bliss.

My life was about to change drastically again because in September I was to start at primary school. At the end of July, just before the summer holiday started, I was allowed to go to school for an afternoon with my sister, just to see what it was like. I was still an avid thumb sucker and my cushion was never very far away. My sister, who didn't like the thought of having to take me in the first place, was walking in front of me. When she turned round to hurry me up, she noticed that I was dragging my cushion behind me. She wasn't just cross, she was hopping. She grabbed me by the hand and dragged me all the way back home. I was so shocked by this that I even forgot to cry.

When my mother saw us coming into the shop she asked, "What are you doing back here?"

"Well, look at this stupid kid, she's going to school with her cushion. Now I'm going to be late and I'll have to run all the way to be on time. I'm not taking this idiot child," and off she ran.

That was the end of my afternoon at school. My mother thought, thankfully, that it was very funny, but did explain to me that when I was going to my new school I couldn't take my cushion. I was a big girl now and I had to start behaving like one and big girls did not go round sucking their thumbs and dragging cushions.

That was dreadful news to me and, however I had been looking forward to going to the 'big' school, the dread of being without my comforter had now put rather a damper on it. What I couldn't make out was that I had been allowed to take it to nursery school.

153

So what was so different, they were both called schools weren't they?

It took a while to get over this shock but from then on I tried very hard to wean myself of my cushion and when September came I happily entered into this new stage of my life.

There was still a terrible shortage of clothes and shoes. My mother, who always made sure that we were turned out well, had knitted vests and knickers from white cotton for me. They must have been the worst garments anybody ever had to endure. The vests were all right but sitting at school all day on wooden benches with hand knitted knickers was a disaster. My whole bottom used to be a pattern of pearl one, knit one and the itching nearly drove me mad. I had to put up with them for quite a long time until more comfortable ones were once again available in the shops.

Our family loved swimming and as soon as it was possible we started going to places near the bigger canals outside the town or to the little inlet of the harbour where I was taught to swim. My mother had knitted me a swimming costume and it was lovely until I went into the water and came out with the crotch hanging somewhere on my knees. The pure weight of it nearly killed me but that was all I had and it was yet again something else I had to get used to.

I learned to swim that first summer in the little inlet of the harbour. I hated to go there because there were tiny crabs in the water that would, I was sure, pinch you while you were swimming. My parents assured me they wouldn't but one day when I was right in the middle of the inlet I could certainly feel a crab on my leg. I started to scream my head off and nearly drowned in the process. As was my parents' normal practice, they were falling about laughing but came to my rescue in the end.

Life was still very exciting for me, because new items were arriving in the shop and I would inspect them all when I came home from school.

Sweets returned and you could buy them with the sugar coupons. My mother would give me my share of the coupons and I could spend them how I liked. I always spent mine in my

154

mother's shop, of course, because if she didn't have the coupons she couldn't get any other stock.

I was allowed to weigh them myself and put them in a little brown bag. The delight of popping one of those brightly coloured treasures into my mouth and sucking it was the height of luxury to me. It was as if I'd moved into a world of plenty. I had never missed those treats because I couldn't remember ever having them. The saying 'what you've never had, you don't miss' was certainly true in my case and that made all those new experiences even better.

I remember the first real chocolates arriving, beautifully packed in a lovely box. The return of these goodies was the best thing that had happened for a long time to the wife of the miller, Mrs Terlaak. The war had been bad enough for her but the absence of sweets a total disaster.

Her husband kept her very short of money and her coupons did not stretch much further than the sugar needed in the household. She was crafty though. My mother knowing her craving used to really tease her.

"Look, Mrs Terlaak, what we've got now, real chocolates with lovely centres."

"Oh, I wish I could buy some," she would say, her mouth watering just by thinking of the taste and the delight of feeling the chocolate on her tongue.

"Well you've got sugar coupons, haven't you?"

"Yes, but my husband will know that I haven't used them on the right things, you know what he's like, mean sod. I tell you what, give me 450 grams of sugar and 50 grams of chocolates, he won't notice that, will he?" She left the shop clutching the few chocolates as if they were the crown jewels. When my mum told the story to my dad, he thought she was awfully cruel and horrible but he was, nevertheless, laughing when he told her off.

"You are horrible, honestly, why did you have to say you had those chocolates?"

"Well, poor woman, she adores sweets. That stupid husband of hers gives her just enough money and coupons for that day and she has to explain when she's a cent short. At least she was happy for half an hour."

"Yes, I know he's not a very nice chap, but I still think you should have kept your mouth shut and not have shown them to her, that was cruel."

"Oh, for God's sake don't make such a song and dance about it. I made her happy and that's much more important. If I didn't need the bloody coupons I would have willingly given her the whole box, poor old soul."

"Yes, I suppose you're right. I bet she sat at home savouring every little bit. I'm sure it put a smile on her face."

Ham had also returned to the shops. The rations were still very small but at least it was available. One day we had a terrible panic in the street. Arend Sluyter, the boy who had been born during the war and was by now four years old, had disappeared. Mrs Sluyter went frantic. She went from house to house asking if anybody had seen him. Nobody had but they all started looking for him. They looked in the fields, in all the other streets but Arend was nowhere to be found.

Mrs Sluyter didn't know what to do with herself and decided to go through the house once more and then she discovered him. He was hiding under her bed with the wrappers from the packet of ham. He had eaten the lot.

Everybody was relieved and had a good laugh about it but I doubt if his father and the other children were very pleased because he had consumed their rations for a whole week.

When winter arrived bringing an abundance of snow with it, I still had no proper shoes to wear so I had to wear wooden clogs. They were lovely and warm and you took them off before you went into the classroom. The problem with them was that snow would pack under them and it became like walking on mini icebergs. Every few metres you had to stand still, lean against a wall and take them off, one at a time, and remove the snow platform. Thank God I only had to wear them for one winter.

All the time things which I'd never seen came back on the market and one day I noticed strange sweets called 'lollipops' in the sweet shop in the market square. I had never seen anything so lovely. Long things on sticks coloured red, yellow and orange. I

156

stood drooling in front of the window. We didn't have those in the shop.

The problem was if I bought them with my sweet rations I would deprive my mother of the coupons. So I decided I would just have to wait until we would get them as well, but I couldn't get them out of my mind though.

At night, in bed, I could just imagine how amazingly lovely they must be. Every time I came over the market square I would stand there and look at them. In the end it became too much and I reluctantly approached my mother.

"Mum, will we get lollipops in the shop soon?"

"I wouldn't have thought so, why?"

"Well, you see, they have them in the sweet shop in the market square and they look really, really lovely."

"I'm sure they do, I suppose you'd really, really like some of them, wouldn't you?"

"Yes Mum, but then you would lose the coupons."

"Oh darling, don't worry about that. I do understand, Mummy really doesn't mind. Poor little darling, you're six years old and never had a lollipop. Mummy will give you the coupons and the money and then you can go and buy them."

I ran to the market as fast as my little legs could carry me and bought them. They were absolutely delicious, but the fact that I had used my coupons in somebody else's shop took some of the pleasure away. It was the first and the last time I bought sweets in somebody else's shop.

When I was seven I had really become too big to be sitting in a little seat on the back of my parents' bikes and they were looking round for an old bike which could be converted for me. Aunt Dit came to the rescue. A friend had given her another bike and I could have hers. Great joy.

The problem was though, that I was only small and the bike was really for a grown up. In those days it was quite normal to have 'blocks' on the pedals. This means thick pieces of wood on either side of the pedal so it was easier to reach them. When you grew a bit, they were removed.

My father had also lowered the handlebars so all should have

157

been well. But it wasn't because I still couldn't reach the pedals. He had the bright idea to take the saddle off and fasten it lower down the bar. That did mean that this bar was sticking out from behind the saddle. Yes I could now reach the pedals but I hated it. It looked absolutely stupid. When my mother came out to look at it she nearly collapsed laughing and that really did it.

"I am not going to ride this stupid bike; look at it, it looks like I've got a drain pipe sticking up behind me."

"Looks more like an anti-aircraft gun," my mother said trying very hard not to laugh again. She really was a great help in circumstances like this.

"What's the matter with it? I've done my best for God's sake, at least she can ride it now," argued my father.

"I'm not riding it because everybody will laugh at me, look at Mum, she's nearly choking."

"No, darling, honestly it will be all right, we'll stick a flag in it, that will make it look better," she said disappearing into the house to have a good chuckle.

I had to ride it, of course, because we had nothing else. At least we could now all go for bike rides to the countryside or the beach. It also made me feel quite grown up and that softened my attitude somewhat.

Slowly but surely everything returned to normal. Health services started to work properly again and for some strange reason lots of children were having their tonsils out. I was no exception. I dreaded it but I was promised a present if I didn't cry.

When we arrived at the clinic there were at least another ten or fifteen children waiting. They were all terrified apart from one girl who I knew vaguely. She piped up that she was certainly not going to cry because only babies cried.

Every child who was seen to before me cried when they came out but she, indeed, didn't. She walked out with her mum without shedding one tear. I hated her from that moment onwards.

It was a terrible experience. You were taken into the treatment room on your own. The mothers or fathers had to wait in the waiting-room. They all had a towel with them to stem the blood after the operation. The nurse tied a rubber apron round you. You then had to sit on her lap, which was also protected by a waterproof apron; just in case a child wet itself, I suppose. The nurse, who was very kind, held your arms behind your back. You were told to open your mouth and snip, snip out came your tonsils, which were dumped in a bucket that stood next to the chair.

The pain was excruciating. No anaesthetic or anything was administered. It sounds barbaric now but that's how it was done. I expect that medicines were still in short supply.

I bawled my eyes out but still received my present a few days later. My mother had to carry me while I was crying and holding the towel against my mouth. Luckily Uncle Arie was having a chat on the bridge and seeing my mother struggle came to our rescue. He took me in his strong, big arms and carried me home. Some of my uncles and aunts and Grandma came to see me and they all brought me a little gift. I must admit that did soften the blow rather a lot.

My mother's youngest brother Tienus had gone back to England to be with his new lady and daughter, but he had to sort out his divorce from his first wife and he also wanted to introduce Aunt Olive and his little daughter to his family, so they came to stay with us for a while before they returned to England for good to live in the Lake District.

It was very exciting, because Aunt Olive only spoke English and I thought it was very posh to have an aunt who only spoke a foreign language. I adored the little daughter, because she was the most beautiful baby I had ever seen. How on earth we managed with all of them in our house I shall never know. They stayed for weeks and weeks and in the end it nearly drove my mother mad.

For me it was wonderful because Aunt Olive had taught me to sing *Ba Ba Blacksheep* and I had to perform this song in all the classes at school. I was very proud of my English aunt and even brought my teacher home one day because she could talk to her in English.

Luckily my mother still spoke a little of the language because of the time she lived in Great Yarmouth when she was a child. I'm quite sure though, that my mother was quite relieved when they left, however much she loved her brother. I only saw my uncle once more, just before my mother died.

The dramatic society had started to rehearse for plays again. The performances were always in the cinema at the end of our road and, as we lived closer by than any of the other members, our house was nearly always stripped bare of furniture on the night of the performance because it all stood on the stage, much to my father's chagrin.

"Oh, bloody hell, why can't somebody else bring some stuff for a change, can't they hire it or something?"

"Oh, shut up, I've left you a chair to sit on, haven't I? It's only for one night and you'll be in the theatre tonight anyway. So stop blooming moaning," my mother would retort.

How we ate our tea at nights like that, I can't really remember, but I suppose we had a picnic in the middle of the living-room floor. My dad always took me and my sister to see the performance, until Dicky became a member herself when she was about sixteen. The first time I was in a play was when I was about eight.

The plays they did were always terribly dramatic and the whole audience would be in tears. It was a good night out for everybody when they could have a good cry. The plays were always about fishing boats lost at sea, or somebody who was handicapped. I used to cry my heart out, particularly when my mother was crying on the stage; much to the annoyance of my dad who would tell me to shut up or he would take me home. That, of course, made me scream even louder. I must have been a terrible embarrassment at times.

Soon after the war finished my father had to start his lessons for his trading licence. My mother would have liked to do this but as the shop was in my dad's name it had to be him. That was hard for him because studying was something very unusual in those days. As soon as they were old enough they had to start work. My father was not stupid but applying his mind to learning wasn't easy. Dirk Pons, the posh gentleman who had helped in the negotiations for the shop and who lived in the posher part of our road taught him. He was the director of the National Health Insurance office in Maassluis.

When the day of the exams arrived my dad was in a state of total panic.

"Mien, I can't do this, it's going to be a disaster."

"Of course you can do it, Dirk Pons said you're doing fine. Don't worry about it. Just go there and do the best you can and if you fail, well, so what, you'll just have to do it again. Nobody will think less of you." And off the poor man went to Rotterdam where the examinations were held.

When, six weeks later, the results came, he had failed all three subjects. He went upstairs. Then we heard an almighty noise. Accompanied by a terrible oath he'd thrown all his books down the stairs. We really did feel so sorry for him, but this gesture was so funny that the three of us just burst out laughing. We certainly were a very sympathetic lot!

Three months later he sat the same exam and passed all three subjects with a ten, the highest marks possible.

A few years later Dirk Pons, who knew my father quite well by now, offered him a job. In those days you could insure yourself, through the National Health, against long periods in hospital. You paid a few cents per week and that was collected by agents. That was the job he was offered. It would mean, however, that we had to move to the village of Maasland a few miles away.

My mother was very keen for my father to improve himself but it was hard to persuade him. He had very little self-confidence and felt that working in a factory was all he could ever achieve. After much discussion and, I might add, rows he took the job.

By then I was ten years old. Life was now so very different. We moved to this lovely house with a front and back garden in a beautiful street with trees on both sides. We had two lovely rooms divided by glass doors that were always open in the summer and French windows in the living-room. The washbasin in one of the two bedrooms was the height of luxury. We still had no bathroom but we did have this wonder of modern hygiene, a flushing toilet. My mother really felt that we'd gone up in the world and she was incredibly proud of her house and very happy.

My sister had finished secondary school and was working and courting her future husband.

The shopping habits of the people were changing and corner shops were already starting to disappear. Ours was probably one of the first to go. It was hard to believe that the war had only been over for four years. We were in the fast lane of change.

I may have been very small during the war but certain things stuck. I still hate wasting food and when my own children would moan about their dinner, my sympathetic answer was always the same: Eat it up because in the war you would have been pleased with it. They still say it themselves and laugh about it. Let's hope they never have to learn the truth of those words.

My Mother's Family During the War Years

Granny Martina van Teylingen, widow of **Eerde van Teylingen**

Gerrit married Riek Prang
Wijnie
Tieny
Riek
Gerda

Eerde married Anne (surname unknown)
Annie
Tieny
Nellie

Wilhelmina (my mum) married Kardien van der Hoek (my dad)
Dicky (my sister)
Wilhelmina (Willy) [myself]

Dirk married Lien Poot
Eerde
Piet
Ria
Willeke

Tienus married Lena Minderhout
Corrie
Nellie

Dirkje (Dit) married Gerrit Bredius
Corrie

Leo (half brother)

Martina (Tieny – half sister)

163

My Father's Family During the War Years

Grandad Kardinus van der Hoek married **Grandma Dirkje van der Hor**

Geertruida (Truus) married Hugo den Hond (died 1943)
Arie
Ditta

Hendrik (Henk – died 1942) married Johanna Verboon
Kardien
Nicolaas

Elizabeth (Bep)

Johannes (Jan) married Anna van den Berg
Dicky
Cornelis (Cor)

Rutger (lived in America) married Elizabeth (surname unknown)
Robert
Elizabeth

Neeltje (Nel) married Harrie Vermeulen
Corrie
Dixie
Nellie
Henrietta (Hannie)

Kardinus (Kardien) [Dad] married Wilhelmina (Mien) van Teylingen [Mum]
Dicky (my sister)
Wilhelmina (Willy) [myself]

Arie married Alida Weijgerse
Kardien
Wilhelmina (Willy)

Adriaan

Johannes (Jo)